Create the LIFE You Dream About

Discover Your Inner Power to Change Your Life

One Woman's Journey from a Small Ukrainian Town to Being a Motivational Speaker in the USA

Anna Simpson

ISBN 978-1-912328-14-7

© 2018 by Anna Simpson. All rights reserved.

This book is copyright under the Berne Convention. All intellectual property rights including copyright, design right and publishing rights rest with the author, Anna Simpson No part of this book may be copied, reproduced, stored or transmitted in any way including any written, electronic, recording, or photocopying without written permission of the author. Although every precaution has been taken to verify the accuracy of the information contained herein, the author and publisher assume no responsibility for any errors or omissions. No liability is assumed for damages that may result from the use of information contained within. Published by Orla Kelly Publishing.

http://anna-simpson.com

Orla Kelly Publishing
27 Kilbrody, Mount Oval,
Rochestown, Cork,
Ireland.

Testimonials

"Anna's book is really inspirational full of personal stories and life lessons she learned while pursuing her dreams and desires. Her journey from poverty in a small Ukrainian village to building her dreams in the USA encourages readers to think bigger and have a big vision for ones life. She shares practical steps and recommendations on how to apply success and achievement principles in order to live a happy and fulfilled life based on her experience. Anna truly walks her talk! If you are dreaming of a bigger and better life, if you wish to find clarity on your purpose, and if you have unexpressed desires and dreams, Anna will show you how to unlock your potential and create the life you dream about."

Paul Martinelli,
West Palm Beach, FL, USA
President of the John Maxwell Team

"Every one of us has a dream. Every soul has its calling. Sadly, so few of us make those dreams a reality. We dismiss them because they're often far removed from the existing conditions and circumstances of life, and it's only at the back end of life that we truly understand the extent of the price we paid. That's why the book you now hold in your hand is one of the most important you'll ever read. This is a real life story of a child born into poverty, surrounded by naysayers. This is a real life story of a child who had a dream that everyone dismissed as fantasy. This is the real life story of a little girl who, against all the odds, became the woman who made that dream a reality.

Every life needs illuminating. Every life needs the inspiration of another life. Every one of us needs that living example to encourage us to be what we could be, to believe in the possibility and our ability to make it happen. Anna brings that illumination to you by sharing the intimate journey of her life from the girl from the small, backwater town in a remote area of a backward country, to the woman standing in front of house, inspiring thousands from the stage in the land of her dreams. Anna is an incredible woman. Assertive, persistent, confident yet caring, she will connect you to a part of yourself you've forgotten...a part of yourself you need more now than ever...the part of yourself where you power to make that dream of yours a reality lies. This book isn't just about the magnificent story, it gives you the practical steps to bring profound improvements to your life. I can promise you, your life will be much richer for reading it."

Christian Simpson

Leading UK business coach, John Maxwell's business associate

"My Dearest Anna,

Wow, what a pleasure it is to know you and to have you in my life! You are a true example of huge success. I know what it is to live in Ukraine and very few have a dream, courage, motivation, desire and take action to actually do something about their life's.

Everything that you had to go through only proofs that YOU are very self-driven, intelligent and smart. Your story and inspiration is now changing life's of others. And You are just getting started. I love your book, quotes, stories and will return to it over and over again. Thank you for walking the walk and leading by example.

As a Ukrainian, I am so proud of you showing the world what Ukrainian Girl can achieve. Your Story is a Glory! You are beautiful inside and out! To Your Great Success!!! Thank you,"

Your Ukrainian friend,

Oxana Dats

Sarasota, FL, USA

Health, Balance, Life Purpose Coach

"It's phenomenal to see how far you can go when you become intentional about designing your life rather than letting it happen to you. This book will help you realise the importance of having a vision for your ideal life. Anna's journey will inspire you to think and dream bigger! Anna, you amaze me, my friend! "

Allison Liddle,

Bestselling **Author** of *"Life Under Construction: Designing a Life You Love,* **Award-Winning Entrepreneur, Speaker**

Wausau, Wisconsin, USA

"Anna Simpson's book "Create the Life You Dream About" opened my self-awareness. I agree with Anna that we have to search for our dream within not outside, just like Hindus legend story says that Anna talks about "Deity in Jeans We Are." Many people are trying to copy success of others, but in the end it doesn't make them happy because it wasn't truly what they wanted to do in life. The book is empowering a reader to follow his/her passion through example of Anna's personal story and achievements. I truly believe that positive set of mind, confidence in yourself and action can lead person to great results. I like Anna's saying "Everyone wants to be Anna Simpson, even Anna Simpson." She said you need to fall in love with yourself and its true!

Everyone has their uniqueness and if we don't love ourselves, we will never embrace it. The book is, also, a helpful guide for people who are in a process of searching their dream. It describes how to identify a dream and pursue it. I am thankful I was introduced to Anna's Simpson book. It was definitely a positive experience and I would encourage everyone to read it who wants to create the life his/her dream about!!

Irina Indiguez

San Diego, CA, USA

Real Estate Agent

"I really enjoyed reading Anna's book. It is very inspirational and encouraging to read about her journey and struggles along the way. I come from Russia myself, so in many ways I could relate to Anna's story and difficulties. Anna's book reminded me that we all can achieve our dreams and ambitions if we put our mind and efforts to it. It encouraged me to believe in more."

Yuliya Georgieva,

Miami, FL, USA

Student, Master in Business Administration in Construction Management

"As a former classmate who knows Anna since she is 7, I haven't been waiting something else from her as such a great book - a book of power, strength and eternal striving for the better world. Remembering her as a bit shy but still ambitious girl, who was reading Daile Carnegie with 12 (really progressive author for a small provincial Ukrainian town to that time by the way) it's still unbelievable what a huge mind-shift she has done since then. Anna is courage enough to tell the world about shortages of own childhood, miss-failures in her relationships or difficulties on the way to success.

Anna's story shows us that new patterns of thinking which open us the doors to a happy life and self-fulfillment are available to us at this very moment and absolutely free of charge. Just listen to your inner voice, stop fitting, follow your biggest dreams and wonder will happen! Bravo, Anna"

Alla Bilenka

Germany

Student, Bachelor in Psychology and Psychotherapy

About The Author

My name is Anna Simpson and I am a personal development teacher, a published inspirational author and an internationally recognised motivational speaker.

I was born in a small Ukrainian town called Polonne, in a poor but loving family. I have always aspired to experience more from life as I knew the world could offer so much more. I refused to accept less and started looking for ways to break way from the life I was living which didn't seem to hold a promising future for me. I made a firm decision to make something of myself and my life.

As a firm believer that people are the creators of their own destiny, I became proactive as opposed to reactive while crafting my life and following my dreams. At first, my ambitions were held together with nothing more than my enthusiasm, but later they acquired flesh and blood, took shape and materialised.

At the age of 21, I fulfilled my dream travelling to the land of opportunities, USA, all by myself. The path was challenging but extremely rewarding. The first couple of years were tough being on my own without help or support.

Holding multiple jobs in customer service that didn't satisfy me emotionally or financially, I developed an insatiable appetite for learning and growing, expanding my mind, and enlarging my awareness in the areas of human development and the psychology of success. Personal growth became my healthy addiction. I didn't have any support starting off, but I desperately needed it.

Then I re-discovered my passion for motivational speaking, which has been within me since childhood, and my purpose being to help women who need the encouragement, support and inspiration to transform their lives.

I joined the John Maxwell team (a global organization of leaders) and have become a transformational teacher and a inspirational speaker.

Now, I am re-engineering my life in the UK and am married to the man of my dreams.

I warmly invite you to connect with me via my website http://anna-simpson.com.

Anna Simpson

To my parents: Helena Cherpakova and Leonid Trishch, my sister Nelia Trishch, and my husband Christian Simpson. I love you and am very grateful to call you family.

Contents

Testimonials iii

About The Author vii

Dedication ix

Preface.. xiii

Introduction... 1

Chapter 1: You Are the Creator 5

Chapter 2: Understanding the Life Force Within You.. 15

Chapter 3: What Is Your Dream? 30

Chapter 4: Only You Can Make Your Dream Life a Reality....... 56

Chapter 5: Find the Meaning of Your Life................... 73

Chapter 6: The Importance of Self-Development 88

Chapter 7: The Operations of Your Mind.................. 100

Chapter 8: Winner's Qualities 108

Last Words 128

Acknowledgements.. 131

References 132

Preface

My dear ladies, There is a whole world within you that is waiting to be discovered and there is a whole world around you waiting for you to create it.

You don't have to dramatically change your life like I did, moving to a different country for example. In fact, the outside changes won't do you justice.

You have to change your mind. There is nothing more powerful than a changed mind. You can change your clothes, you can change your hair, your spouse, your place of residence. But the same experiences will perpetuate themselves until you change your mind.

If you wish to get out of struggle and mediocrity, you need to look within. You need more confidence, but it also has to come from within you and be allowed to grow. I believe that life is not about resources; it is about resourcefulness.

> **Your personality is the resource for everything you have and are going to have.**

Do you have the following qualities for success yet still feel trapped?

√ A woman who has a hungry and open mind

√ Curiosity driven, who is willing to learn and grow

√ Determined and hard-working

√ Serious and willing to change

√ A business-owner or a commissioned driven professional

√ A desire to be and have more

Can you identify with any of the above important attributes for success but yet are you still struggling with relationships, a job that seems to suck the life out of you, a life that seems to lack luster and ever mounting frustration that you are stuck in a rut?

I am speaking here to every woman who knows in their gut and in their heart that they can be, do and have more but just don't know how. Believe me, you can do it! You are more than enough!

How can I be so sure when I don't know you personally and how can I be sure I can even help?

You see we have more in common than you think. I had all of these positive attributes but was getting nowhere. In fact there were so many times I began to question my life's purpose, my worthiness, my potential. The only things I had in abundance were limiting beliefs and I felt crushed.

When you see how I turned my life around and take on board and practice the strategies I share with you, you too can **discover your inner power to change your life.**

Remember, these same practices and strategies are available to you right here right now.

They took me from poverty in a small Ukrainian town where English was not my mother tongue to realising my dream of coming to the USA and becoming an American citizen, being married to the man of my dreams, living the "pinch me" type of lifestyle and doing what I love which is empowering and inspiring other women.

It is my mission in life to help women gain self-confidence and self-belief in their potential, unique gifts and capacities, to help them understand that they can achieve their goals, dreams and aspirations and can enjoy their dream life in personal and professional areas.

There are so many women who are questioning their worthiness and capabilities, but they remain stuck in their comfort zone rather than having faith in themselves and confidence and courage to pursue their dreams. They settle for less in their careers or stuck in jobs they despise. They don't believe they are enough and worthy to attract their dream man, or they have another limiting belief that all great men are taken. It doesn't have to be this way. Read on and I will show you how!

Introduction

Dear reader, it is my sincere hope that this book will inspire you to believe in yourself and gain the courage to pursue your dreams and heart-felt desires, so you can live your dream life. We all deserve to live the life we dream about.

I love dreaming. And although it might sound quite bold, I discovered that if I *really* want that dream, I can make it a reality. You're probably wondering *how?* Even more likely, you probably doubt that it's possible. That's fair, because it is a bold statement, so in this book I'll share my story with you, along with some of the important lessons I've learned along the way. Through this book, you'll see that not only did I make my dreams a reality, but you can do the same.

If you are not enjoying your current conditions and circumstances, if you feel there is something missing in your life, if it seems like life is a continuous struggle, or if you believe there is more to life: more satisfaction, more freedom, more happiness, more prosperity, and more fulfilment, then this book is for you.

I am honoured to share with you my life's journey—from a small Ukrainian town where I grew up in a poor family to creating my dream life in the USA, to now enjoying a happy life in the beautiful English countryside (as my American friends say, in "a royal country"), being married to the man of my dreams, frequently travelling around the world, and loving what I do.

My goal is to inspire you to think bigger and build a bigger vision for your dream life—and to gain the confidence and self-belief that you **can** achieve it. This book will give you tools and strategies on how you can make your dream life a reality.

If you want to transform your business life, create more profit and freedom, and be able to make better lifestyle choices, this book is for you. If you want to improve your personal relationships and your family life, or you wish to attract your soulmate, this book is also for you. This book is for anyone who isn't living their dream life, perhaps doesn't even know what their dream life is, but *really wants to*.

In this book, I'll show you how to identify and gain clarity on what your dreams are. I'll teach you how to believe in yourself by accepting the ultimate truth that you are the creator of your own life. We'll awaken your "let's go!" mentality. You'll find the true meaning of your life. You'll discover how to grow and develop yourself so that what you think, say, do, and create are in harmony. You'll also find out the winner's qualities you need to cultivate within yourself to live a successful and happy life.

As a motivational speaker, it breaks my heart to see so many talented, gifted, and capable people living mediocre lives. There are many reasons why, but their underlying belief is often that they don't believe they can live their dream life. They have no self-confidence, and so they have settled for less. They'd prefer to live a life of comfort and familiarity, rather than a life of promise and the unknown. They live by the principle: *the better the devil you know*. Very often, they seem stuck like this.

Despite being discontent, many people feel safe where they're stuck, and this is why they don't make any changes. They have mistakenly bought into their limiting beliefs that only a few "lucky" people can enjoy their dream life, or that life is already predetermined by destiny, or that they lack certain talents or skills, or any other BS (bogus story) they have chosen to accept as the truth. They refuse to take responsibility for all the conditions and circumstances they experience in their life. They don't realise that *they* are the cause of every single effect in their life.

The vast majority of people do not realise they are in a constant process of creation. Unfortunately, for most people, this process is unconscious: they don't pay attention to their thoughts, yet their thoughts influence their behaviours. For you to enjoy the fruits of creation, the creative process has got to be intentional: your thoughts, your words, and your actions have to be aligned.

But you don't have to be one of those people. Life doesn't have to be mediocre. You can take control of your own life and start creating the life you really want, not the average one you've settled for. So, I'd like to invite you on an exciting journey of self-development that will enable you to create the life you dream about.

Before we begin, I'm going to ask you to unlock your imagination—the one you had as a child, then shut away at the back of your grown-up mind. I'm going to ask you to throw common sense to the wind and pretend you are that child again…

Do not think for a moment that your dream or aspiration is impossible, because even the word itself says "I'm possible!" Throw your doubts, limiting beliefs, and judgment to the wind, allow yourself to get inspired and motivated, and give yourself permission to think bigger for your life.

Anna Simpson

Do you remember the Arabian tales known as *One Thousand and One Nights?* When I was a child, I used to watch the Aladdin's lamp cartoon repeatedly. There was something magical about the story that really captivated my mind. All you have to do is rub it and the mighty genie appears, ready to carry out your three wishes. I believe that all of us have longed to get our hands on that magic lamp at one time or another. Well I'm here to tell you that you do possess a magic lamp and it's not limited to just three wishes!

Now it's time to grab hold of this powerful force within you. Once you decide to awaken that inner power, you'll be unstoppable in creating mental, emotional, physical, financial, and spiritual abundance beyond your wildest fantasies. Whether your dreams materialise instantly or take shape gradually, the only limit on what you can have in your life is the size of your imagination and the level of your commitment to make your dreams reality.

CHAPTER 1

You Are the Creator

You are more powerful than you think you are. You have the power to achieve anything you desire if you recognise the creator within you.

Everyone has all of the resources they need to succeed and achieve their desired outcome. We were all filled with wonder, excitement, determination, and enough energy at one point in our lives. If you look at any 4-year-old, you will see all of those traits and more. We were all 4-year-olds at one point, and we had all of those traits. However, as we got older, through our experiences, messages from other people, and limiting beliefs, we closed the doors on the behaviours that can bring us our desired outcomes.

We seem to have lost touch with our true and powerful selves. We fail to recognise the powerful creator within us. We settle for less, because we are afraid to dream of more. We say "I don't know how. I don't have the time, money, or resources. I don't think I have what it takes," and we come up with a million other excuses not to pursue our vision. And the only thing worse than an excuse is a good excuse. Don't we all have a bunch of those "good" excuses? "Yes," you might say, "but my situation is different."

Everybody's situation and story is different—but that's not an excuse to not pursue your dreams. Let me share a bit of my simple but unique life story that I hope will inspire you to aspire for more in your life.

Where you're from doesn't define who you are

I was born and raised in a small, poor town called Polonne in the Khmelnytski region in the Central West of Ukraine (you might have heard this said as "the Ukraine", but the correct way to say it is "Ukraine"). People from the USA often ask me what it's like to live in Ukraine and I always tell them it is hard. I come from a very modest background with exceedingly limited resources and a widespread victim psychology. Let me tell you, small Ukrainian towns are not fun at all. Things that are taken for granted in the USA are considered luxuries in my home town. Our situation was even worse, as my family belonged to the lower class. My parents worked very hard but could barely make ends meet. We often didn't have enough money to buy food. Thankfully, we had chickens, turkeys, and geese, and a garden with fruit and vegetables.

My sister and I used to wait with anticipation for my aunt and uncle to visit us once a year. They were exciting moments for us, and our parents as well. My aunt and uncle would always bring delicious presents from the big city—Saint Petersburg. They bought chocolates, vegetables and exotic fruits such as mandarins, mangos, grapes, oranges, and avocados—foods that we were unfamiliar with, and quite frankly didn't know what to do with. They bought us assortments of cheese and tasty sauces—things that people in the USA take for granted. Those times were holidays for us, because we couldn't afford to buy any of those items, and even if we could, many of them weren't available to buy in our town.

We had running water, but only because we had to run for it! We didn't have hot or cold running water inside our home. We didn't have a toilet inside the house either. So if we had to go to the toilet at night, no matter whether there was rain, hail, snow, or it was freezing cold, we had to go outside.

My family was poor—and we knew it. My sister and I were fortunate to have loving and caring parents, but unfortunate to experience the pain of a poor life. There were many challenging times because of our family's economic situation. I still remember children at school laughing at my old clothes. I always felt embarrassed when my classmates were discussing some of the popular TV shows or new movies, as we couldn't afford a TV so I couldn't join in the conversation. Often, I felt humiliated because of our poverty.

When I was about 8 years old, I wanted my parents to buy me a bicycle. All of my friends on our street had one, and they had fun riding together. People in Ukraine live in communities and the kids always play together. However, my parents couldn't buy me a bicycle—not because they didn't want to, but because they couldn't afford it. If you think about it, a bike isn't a big deal, but in my child mind, it was a huge deal. When you are young, you tend to exaggerate things, so I felt rejected and incomplete. I felt inadequate. I wondered what made my friends better than me so they could have a bike. I questioned my self-worth. I couldn't understand what my friends had that I didn't. That's tough for an 8-year-old.

My mom saw my struggle and said, "Honey, we love you, but you have to understand." And I did understand that life wasn't fair. There were many times of lack in my childhood that made me think life was unfair and painful. However, much later in my life, I realised that my personal worthiness is not defined by material possessions. It is not about resources—but rather resourcefulness.

It doesn't matter what you have; it matters who you are. If you don't have something today, you might get it tomorrow. That story about the bike planted the seed of learning for me that your outside circumstances should not define who you are, but my acceptance of that truth happened much later. No matter where you are, you are there, but your personal value shouldn't be defined by that place.

Don't get me wrong, I'm not against material things and wealth. But I believe that your character, heart, and soul are so much more important than any pleasure that material things can offer. Meanings and value are in people, not in things. I love my parents dearly and I'm grateful to them for bringing my sister and I up with absolute love and care. I believe that our parents did a great job of raising us. They wanted to give us the world. It's a shame they couldn't. But that didn't matter, because they gave us so much more instead.

Find inspiration in desperation

The hardships from my childhood made me hungry and eager to create a better, more abundant, and more fulfilled life. For me, this was the inspiration through my desperation. Later in life, I found those difficult moments were gifts in disguise, diamonds in the rough, treasure in the trash. They helped me shape my personality and a winner's leadership edge within me. My story of poverty became my story of empowerment. I learned many lessons from life's hardships. I learned that *you grow when you experience pain.* You stretch yourself, expand your capabilities, try, fail, pick yourself up, learn, and keep going, and before you know it, you've accomplished something and achieved something.

In my case, it all started with the decision to set my mind on higher and better things in life. What was around me at the time was way too depressing. My parents' life philosophy was simple but not really motivating: *every person's life path is predetermined by destiny and you cannot do anything other than accept it.* I refused to accept that truth. It didn't sound true to me anyway.

Even though our parents loved my sister and I dearly, we lacked an emotional connection with them. We weren't able to open up to them and have a heartfelt conversation about things that had been bothering us or interested us.

My dad is an educated man with an amazing sense of humour and a big heart, but he has deep-seated self-worth issues. He never believed in himself and his capabilities, which put a major lid on his life achievements. A lot of his friends used to ask him, "If you are so smart, why are you so poor?" I came to understand later in my life that poverty and limitations are a product of our mind. He is a great dad and a great husband, but his own limitations were the reason why he was often unhappy and kept to himself.

My mom is a kind-hearted and caring woman. She has many endearing qualities, but being a devout Pentecostal believer, there were many restrictions in our house. She is an uneducated lady, who lived her entire life in a village, so she was easily brainwashed by a strict religious persuasion. Her view on life was very limited and ascetic for religious reasons. I could never have a deep conversation with her about anything other than God or the Bible. Matters such as sex and relationships were never discussed in our family.

Money was considered to be the root of all evil and the devil's plan to destroy humanity. Our mom never encouraged us to study, grow, and develop ourselves so we could do better in life, because she passionately believed that the end of the world was near, so why bother about the mundane and perishable? She was always talking about heaven and how great it would be there and how our physical experience is only transitionary.

When we were little, mom forced us to go to evening meetings with her to celebrate the Holy Spirit. I am not against religion, but I am against ignorance that puts a lid on our lives. I never shared my mom's view on life and things. We loved each other and there was never hostility between us, but we weren't ever able to understand each other, let alone connect at a deep emotional level. Part of me is grateful for those numerous childhood restrictions, because they inspired me to think.

Shoot for the stars

As a child, I was encouraged to dream of more by my beloved grandmother. She was an intelligent and strong woman, who survived World War II and faced many challenges in her life. She was always strongly against my mother's ways of bringing up children in renunciation of life's enjoyment and happiness. So, she would do whatever she could to plant the seeds of greatness within us. Granny always encouraged us to have aspirations for a better life and to have a stellar mindset. "Shoot for the moon, as even if you miss, you will be among the stars," she would say.

Our granny believed in us and so we started believing in ourselves as well. She was an Alpha female and was instrumental in influencing and motivating her granddaughters to have higher demands of life. She was a woman of higher awareness. She didn't have much in life, but she wanted a better future for her beloved granddaughters. Our granny passed away in December 2015, but she is always in my thoughts and my heart. I will always be grateful for her.

When I was 12 years old, I went to my mom and said, "Mom, when I grow up, I want to live in the USA!" She said, "What?! Are you out of your mind?!!" My mom thought I had gone crazy. "It's impossible!" she finished. Somewhere deep inside, I knew that the world was much bigger and could offer much more than my small town could. Let me share with you, when someone tells you that your dream is impossible, it means that it is *worth pursuing*.

My inner hope was sprouting on the surface. My inner spirit was seeking higher expression. I dared to dream, I dared to create a vision bigger than my circumstances. The world is large and small at the same time. So, I started looking for the key to unlock that bigger world. I had nothing, yet everything I needed was within me. Without having anything, I started creating everything—first in my mind. At the beginning, my ambitions were held together by bare enthusiasm, but later they acquired 'flesh and blood.'

Having a curious nature, I asked many questions about life, happiness, contentment, and dreams. I started reading books and creating my own dreams. I wondered whether we could control our destiny. I understood and realised that I could not change my start in life, as my background will always remain the same but I could change my future.

I really love my parents, but their philosophy had nothing to do with ambitions, success, a life of achievement, or a life of greatness. It was so frustrating, because they didn't even believe that they could have a better life. It seemed easier for them to be the victim of their circumstances, but in the long run, a life like this isn't worth living. Despite coming from this past, something inside me whispered that I could change my present and my future.

I stepped up for that dream. I took ownership of it. And it wasn't easy. I would travel hundreds of miles away from my home town to Kyiv and Saint Petersburg, working in restaurants during the summer holidays, waiting on tables, and saving every penny. I didn't enjoy those jobs, but I was determined, and I had a goal ahead of me. It took me close to three years to collect the thousands of dollars necessary to pay for my trip to America. It was a fortune in Ukraine!

Ukraine is a beautiful country, but it's hard to live there, especially if you have big dreams. I faced another big problem—a visa. To say it was complicated is an understatement. I had to collect a whole bunch of paperwork with different documents proving that I am a good citizen, have never committed a crime, have sufficient funds, have a medical certificate to say that I'm healthy, have insurance (which was a pain, as in Ukraine, we rarely do insurance), and proof that I love my country and will come back.

I also had to pay a substantial amount of money to an agency that was arranging the paperwork and submitting the application to the U.S. embassy. It was almost 'mission impossible'. My parents neither supported me nor—thankfully—intruded. They just thought I was crazy and was simply wasting my time. People from our small town didn't usually go further than Kyiv. But I didn't care. When you have a dream, you have a dream, and you go after it. I believed in myself and in my dream, and that was what mattered.

The big day came—my interview day with the U.S. consulate. I have always been confident communicating with others. But that day, I was visibly nervous. Maybe because it was my life-defining moment. Or maybe because the consulate only spoke English. I learned English at college, but I wasn't fluent and had never spoken to a native speaker before. I didn't know what questions the consulate would ask me, so I couldn't prepare for it.

I was scared. There was a long line in front of me. The wait felt like eternity. I saw a few people come back from the interview with sad faces, which didn't seem like a good sign. I don't pray, but if I did, I would have been praying back then.

Then it was my turn.

"What is the purpose of your visit to the USA?" came the first question from a very serious-looking consul. His moustache made him look gruesome.

"To work and to travel," was my eloquently descriptive answer. That was the type of visa I was applying for: a J1 work and travel visa. I tried to smile, but it appeared more awkward than lovely.

There was no reaction on his face. "Do you have any friends or family in the USA?"

"No."

"Do you know where you are going to live in NJ?"

"Yes, in Ocean City." I had no idea where exactly I was going to live. All I cared about was getting there. One step at a time.

"Thank you, ma'am. You are free to go." He put my stack of papers together with my passport.

That's it? I thought. I felt relief and uncertainty. Was I approved for a U.S. visa or not?! I didn't know, because they don't tell you. You find out when you get your passport back.

Anna Simpson

Needless to say, on 3rd May 2010, I landed in JFK Airport, New York. I had come to the land of opportunities. I had fulfilled my dream. I could barely contain myself. My joy didn't have any limits. What I understood was that if you really want something, you can get it, as long as you pay the price.

Bear in mind that at the time, my dream seemed impossible and extremely hard to reach. I had shot for the stars and reached them. However, the fact that I managed to fulfil my dream doesn't make me better or more special than you. *You are the creator of your life.* You need to trust me that you *can* create your dream life. So now you know how I achieved my first big dream, let's look at the creative process.

CHAPTER 2
Understanding the Life Force Within You

As stated earlier, I am not religious. However, I do believe in the spiritual side of our existence. To clarify, whenever I mention the word "God," "spirit," or "divine" in this book, I am **not** referring to man-made theological constructions of these things. My spiritual understanding of the world has nothing to do with the conventional understanding of faith, belief in God, the remission of sins, salvation, or any other beliefs specific to one religion or another. This is my map of the world—I do not impose it on anyone else, and I respect other people's religious beliefs. What I **am** referring to is your spirit: **the life force within you that enables you to exist on a higher level of consciousness**. This is the universal truth of how a human being was created.

In one of my reflections on life and indeed my reflections on myself, I came to understand that I don't end with the limits of my body, and neither does anyone else. From this, I became fascinated with the non-physical part of our being. Let me ask you this: how can one be inspired if they don't recognise the spiritual side of themselves? "Inspired" means "being in spirit". It doesn't matter which theological construction you follow or whether you are an atheist. If you wish to transform your life, you have to recognise **the life force** within you.

If you are pursuing your dream or you are trying to understand what you could do to transform your life, don't look outside of yourself. **Look within you.** My husband always says, "If you fail to go within, you will go without." That's where your life force is found. Your value is not found outside of you.

> *"What lies in front of you and what lies behind you pales in comparison with what lies within you."* – **R. W. Emerson**

I love this quote because it summarises our nature. It helps us recognise our unconditional value and worthiness as human beings.

Do you realise how special and unique you are? It's not your fingerprints or your spiral of DNA that makes you exceptional. Your worthiness is your birth right. You don't need to earn it or come to deserve it. It is already given. You are enough. You are whole and complete, simply because you were born. It is simply a matter of realising who you really are. Your true self contains every possibility. You carry a divine sparkle within you.

This became clear to me when my mother taught us that God created people in his image. Her understanding was that God knows what is best for us, so we can always rely on him in our joy or sorrow. However, my perception of this was: since God is the almighty creator, and since God created all human beings in its image, this means we all have that power as well. This understanding shaped my self-image, and influenced my thoughts, behaviour, and actions.

I truly believe that the universe wants us to be the co-creators of our life. Whether you believe in God or not, the universe or ultimate intelligence wants you to create your life. It doesn't want you to be a bystander in your life. So, when you're writing your life story, don't let anybody hold your pen.

If you doubt this, think about it this way. Every day, we have to make decisions in order to live our life, otherwise we would die. We have to make the decision to eat, to get a job, to earn money. We have to make choices every day, and our choices also affect other people, so the universe wants us to intentionally live our lives. For example, try for a day to not be in control of your own life and not make decisions—you wouldn't get far!

There is a power that animates, penetrates, motivates, and fills the entire cosmos. It brings everything to life. Everything you see around you is an expression of that power. It is everywhere. We sometimes call that power "energy". It is neither created, nor can it be destroyed. It is evenly present in all places, at all times. And that means it's also inside of you. Everything comes from one source and that source, that power, always flows to you and through you. You are that power, that energy. You are a part of the universe and your life is a self-expressive universe.

> The universe is seeking a grander expression through you. It is seeking to express its wonder through you. The same power that rises the sun, blows the winds, pushes the waves of the ocean, makes the buds of flowers bloom, and governs the entire universe is present within you. How do you know that? Because you are being pulled by your inner desires for something more and bigger, even if they are not clear enough yet. This power that pulls and pushes you to a higher and grander expression of yourself is the power of the universe.

You have this power to create and innovate in your life. You just need to train your mind to see great things in the seed before the flower appears, look at the bigger picture, and see the true meaning of things. That's what this book will help you do.

You are the creator of your life

You are the grand expression of the powerful universe. This is a mind-boggling statement, but it's incredibly empowering once you comprehend it. Think about it! If you understand this, you'll understand that **you are the creator of your life.** The power to attain everything you desire is *within you*. Success, achievement, and happiness are not things you pursue; they are things you *are*.

> **Take a moment now and consider your current circumstances—your physical condition, your emotional condition, your possessions, your financial condition, where and how you live, how happy you are. Those are the mirrors showing you who you really are. The universe doesn't give you what you want; it gives you who you are.**

"What you are speaks so loudly that I can't hear what you are saying."
– Emerson

It is your inner world that makes the process of creation possible. Think of artists. They create something out of nothing. It is not the brush, paint, and canvas they use. It is their thoughts, feelings, and imagination that create beauty and art. It is not a material substance with measurable material quantities. What about authors? It is not a pen and paper or a computer and a keyboard. It is their inner world that they transfer through their creations, evoking feelings in their readers.

However, you don't have to be an artist or an author to create something (you can if that's your dream of course). I certainly don't consider myself "creative" in the conventional meaning, but I have written this book as it is part of my dream. I have embraced the fact that *my story is my glory*. I want to let the world know about the power of their dreams, which is linked to their personal power. I want to show people, through my own life example, that they are the creators of their life.

> **Are you living your life in a way that you can say "my story is my glory?" Take a pen and paper and write it down whether you consider your story as your glory and why. Take a moment to write down whether you recognise yourself as the creator of your life and why you think so or not. Don't be discouraged if some areas of your life don't work the way you want right now. Watch your tone, energy, and emotions as you are evaluating your life. Be present during this exercise and be open to any insights.**

> **When you've finished writing, ask yourself the questions:** *What did I learn about myself? What is it I desire in life? What beliefs do I need to make it happen? What's stopping me changing my life? What do I need to overcome it?* **There are no right or wrong answers. Even if your answers don't make you feel good right now, by evaluating your life, you are on the path of transformation.**

The uniqueness of being

To help you better understand your value and the worthiness of your life's journey, let's take a look at the world we live in. Look at nature. Isn't it impeccable and flawless? The creation of the universe is perfect. Have you noticed that every time you are face to face with nature, you feel content? Nature is silent, but it talks to those who listen. When we perceive the mighty ocean, a peaceful lake, an evergreen forest, endless meadows, and an unlimited sky, it fills our heart. You embrace the smells, sensations, and scenery. You feel great, because the power of nature reminds you of your own power, as you are part of it all. This knowledge brings you back in sync with the energy of the universe.

Have you ever seen anything more amazingly perfect than a snowflake? Its intricacy, its design, its symmetry, its conformity to itself, and originality from all else. You wonder at the miracle of this awesome display of nature. Yet, you don't see yourself this way. If a single snowflake is this perfect and unique, what about the universe and every human being? You are unique and perfect like the snowflake.

I'm not talking about your talents and gifts here (though of course you have these), or your material possessions, social status, outstanding results, impressive achievements, or being an amazing wife or a great husband. All of these things matter and define the quality of your life. However, they are more *side effects* of who you really are, which flows into what you do and what you create. These external things fall into place in your best interests **when you become connected to your true self**. What I am talking about is the uniqueness that you get as your birth right—your worthiness as a human being regardless of your achievements or possessions.

You might have heard people say, "Fall in love with yourself" and they are right. Believe it or not, your body loves you unconditionally. What is the proof of this, you ask? Without any effort on your part, your heart is beating, your lungs are breathing, and the rhythm of your life is graciously flowing through you for every day of your life—unconditionally and unconsciously. Think about it. You've got to love yourself just like your body loves you.

> **I am often approached at my seminars and workshops by women who say either they would like to be me or they would like to do what I do. But I always respond, "The last thing you want is be me." Understand, being you is where your power is. Trying to be someone else will undermine your power. Maximise each day of your life and acknowledge even the smallest victories.**

We all have roles models, people we look up to, people we follow, but please don't compare yourself to others, especially those who have achieved a higher level than you. Don't try to be like them—be you! Recognise your unique talents and gifts and take pride in them. You have to take pride in being you, because there is no one else like you. There is only one of you, and there will only be one of you in all time; this expression is unique. If you block it, it will never exist through any other medium. It will be lost, and the world won't have it.

> **For your life to be changed according to your dreams and visions, you need to wholeheartedly believe in yourself. If you believe in your dreams, they might come true. But if you believe in yourself, they will come true. Outside events and circumstances have no power—other than the power you give them. You possess all the power to make the necessary changes in your life.**

Once you realise that you are whole, enough, and complete, your internal transformation will begin. And that will begin to change everything in your life.

"The change begins in our beingness not in our doingness." – **Mahatma Ghandi**

Self-knowledge is power

I'd like to tell you one of my favourite stories from Eckhart Tolle's book *The Power of Now*. There was a beggar who had been sitting by the side of a road for many years. One day, a stranger passed by. The beggar asked the stranger for some spare change. The stranger replied that he didn't have any change, but he asked what the beggar was sitting on. The beggar had been sitting on an old box for as long as he could recall. The stranger asked what was inside it. The beggar said he'd never looked in the box, assuming there was nothing in it. The stranger told him to look inside. When he did, he was shocked to find that the box was full of gold.

Do you realise the meaning of this story? This tale reveals the importance of having self-knowledge of who we really are and what we are capable of. We have to discover the treasure hidden inside us, and we can do this by simply opening the box.

> **Here are some things to think about:**
> - How aware are you about your creative powers?
> - How intentional are you in shaping your own life?
> - What kind of thoughts are mostly in your mind?
> - What are your aspirations?
> - What do you believe about life, the universe, or about yourself?
> - What would living your life to the fullest look like?

Do not underestimate your personal power. You are not just flesh, bones, blood, and intellect. You are a spiritual being having a human experience. Claim your inherent right of being the creator. That is who you truly are. You have to understand that you *can* do it. You can transform your life. You can create your dreams. You were created out of greatness to live a life of greatness. Life isn't just about discovering yourself—it is about creating yourself.

> **Ask yourself,** *who am I?* **That is the most important question you can ask yourself. Your answer will determine the quality of your life. You need to identify yourself, your strengths and weaknesses, your dreams and aspirations, your beliefs, and your struggles. You need to understand yourself. If you know the wisdoms of the world but you don't know yourself, then you know nothing. When contemplating these important self-searching questions, remember your inherent birth right of being the creator of your life.**

Finding your divine power

Have you ever had glimpses of inspiration—when you felt so powerful that you could do anything? Maybe this feeling was triggered by hearing a song you love, or reading an inspirational book, or accomplishing a difficult project? These moments are indicators or reminders of the fact that you are more powerful than you think you are.

There is an interesting Hindu legend about a time when men were gods. Eventually, men started abusing their divine power. Brahma, the chief god, decided to punish men by depriving them of their divinity and hiding it where it could never be found. The question was—where to find the secret place to hide the divinity? So Brahma called a council of the gods to help him decide.

"Let's bury it deep in the earth," said the gods. But Brahma answered, "No, that will not work because humans will dig into the earth and find it."

Then the gods said, "Let's sink it in the deepest ocean." But Brahma said, "No, not there, for they will learn to dive into the ocean and will find it."

Then the gods said, "Let's take it to the top of the highest mountain and hide it there." But once again Brahma replied, "No, that will not do either, because they will eventually climb every mountain and once again take up their divinity."

Then the gods ran out of ideas and said, "We do not know where to hide it, because it seems that there is no place on earth or in the sea that human beings will not eventually reach."

Brahma thought for a long time and then said, "Here is what we will do. We will hide their divinity deep in the centre of their own being, for humans will never think to look for it there."

All the gods agreed that this was the perfect hiding place, and the deed was done. And since that time humans have been going up and down the earth, digging, diving, climbing, and exploring—searching for something already within themselves.

> **The greatness is hidden within you. You have to peel away the layers of self-doubt, self-judgment, fear, and self-limiting beliefs to uncover your amazingness.**

Do not be mistaken, the term "divinity" does not carry a religious connotation here. It refers to the unbridled power of human beings, which makes them the creators and the transformers of their own lives.

There is no such thing as destiny

Whether you realise it or not, you are already in a constant and uninterrupted process of creation. Unfortunately, for the most part, it is an unconscious process. People often don't grasp that they are the creators of their life, and instead they attribute the things that happen to them as "destiny" or "luck" or some other external force.

However, there is no such thing as a predetermined destiny, even though it can feel true for those who believe in it, like my parents. Their reality was designed by their limiting life philosophy that you cannot change your life—you can only learn to adapt to it. The way we perceive the world determines how we live in it. My parents are very nice people, but all of their life, they have struggled, because they don't realise that the limitation and lack exists only in their consciousness.

Predetermined destiny is a man-made concept. And it sets people in a trap. People are born, they exist, and they die without understanding what life is really about. That is the sad reality of the majority people on this earth. These are the people who live their life by default not by design. That would have been my "destiny" too had I not claimed the right of being the creator of my life and been inspired to live my dreams.

> **Suspend the thought "Life happens to me" and develop the attitude "I happen to life!"**

You have that divine presence in your life as well. You don't need to connect to it or go looking for cosmic alignment. It is already part of who you are. You just need to become aware of it. We are already connected. We are a small part of the big whole. Divine presence is within you. It is part of you. It's like your hand—you don't have to connect to it; it is already connected to your body, ready to serve you at any given moment.

You aren't "destined" for a great or a mediocre life. You can choose the life you want to live, and an infinite realm of possibilities is always around you. It is how you use your personal power that brings the results you get, and therefore the life you live. This power can only bring to you what it can bring *through* you. This means you need to be in harmonious vibration with the things and people you want to attract in your life; in other words, your personal energy has to be aligned with your desired outcome for your desires to come to you. To do this, you need to get in tune with yourself.

For example, if a woman has a desire to attract love in her life, she has to **be** love, be loving, have an energy of love within her, love herself, and love the world around her. If she emits the vibrations of love in this way, she will attract love. If her energy is hateful, she hates herself, and hates the world, then she won't attract love. That's the law: like attracts like.

"You are not a drop in the ocean. You are the entire ocean in a drop."
– Rumi

Get in tune with yourself

One way you can get better in tune with yourself is through meditation. I love meditating. I'm not sure whether I do it the right way. I probably don't, but that doesn't matter. I don't always get spiritual revelations and cosmic insights. But I truly enjoy the process of meditation. Being quiet, being at peace with my inner self, and listening to soft relaxing music is very appealing. It has a huge positive impact on my inner harmony.

However, I certainly don't connect with some super powerful outside forces out there, "cosmic energy" as it's overly referred to nowadays. I know this energy is within me. I don't need to go outside of me in order to realise my personal power. I need to become *connected with me*. That's the beauty of meditation for me. If you ever have to connect with anything, it's you. Connect with you! Your feelings, your emotions, your dreams!

> **Try being quiet. I promise you will discover something new and exciting within yourself or will gain an insight or solution to a problem that has been bothering you.**

Summary

You are much more powerful than you think you are. You are a part of the universe. But at the same time, you are a self-expressed universe yourself—who has the power to influence, change, and create the conditions and circumstances of your life. In order to accept this truth, you need to comprehend the spiritual aspect of your being, the life force within you, and the uniqueness of you. Embrace your truth. The truth that you are the creator of your life. That the infinite realm of possibilities is there for you.

The moment you claim the right of being the creator is the moment when you take control of the process of creating your life—your dream life. It is an empowering moment when you tell yourself "I can do this". You begin living intentionally, consciously choosing your thoughts, actions and behaviour. Consequently, your life will start to unfold—not by default, but by design. Understanding your power of being the creator of your life is the first step on the way to creating your dream life.

CHAPTER 3

What Is Your Dream?

"When the dream is right for the person and the person is right for the dream, the two cannot be separated from each other." – John Maxwell

Once you realise you are the creator of your life and embrace the creative life force within you, you need to channel that energy in the right direction by creating a compelling vision or cherished dream that you wish to pursue. Creating a dream is a journey of self-discovery, and it might seem challenging at times, but it is absolutely rewarding in the end.

When we were children and people asked us what we wanted to do with our life, everything seemed possible. There were no limits. When you were little, you created your dreams based on your genuine aspirations, not on your rational thinking. Children have no problem saying, "When I grow up, I'll be an inventor, a famous actress, an astronaut, a world champion footballer, or the president of my country."

Their dreams inspire them and separate them from the limits imposed by their daily routine. But then their parents say, "No, you can't do that. Get real!" What is real anyway? Who gets to define "real?" Or someone says, "That's not normal!" *Real, normal*...there is no such thing. Normal is an illusion. What is normal for a spider is chaos for a fly. Embrace life again, like you did as a child. Choose a dream life based on your real aspirations, not on what somebody told you was possible or "normal".

In this chapter, I'll show you how to identify your dream life. First, I'll tell you how my dream life evolved and the challenges you face when finding your dream.

The land of opportunities

When I reached the USA, even though I had come to the land of opportunities, I soon realised that none of those opportunities were just handed to me or came easy to me. In Ukraine, people used to say that the streets in America were paved with gold. Let me tell you, when I got to America, I quickly found out three things. Number one, the streets were not paved with gold. Number two, the streets were not paved at all. And number three, I was expected to pave those streets. Well, I was expected to pave the streets of my own life. And I did. I paved them really hard, at times working at two or three jobs simultaneously.

I was a young girl having finished college with no real job or professional experience except for waitressing. As much as I didn't like serving jobs, it seemed like one of the few options for me to make money and have fun back then. I have always liked people, so serving in the USA felt kind of cool at the beginning. I can't say that I liked the job itself, but I certainly liked the cash it was generating, which was far more than back home, and I liked immersing myself in American culture.

Anytime I saw a "hiring" sign in a restaurant or café, I checked the opportunity. At one time, I was working three jobs with almost no days off. I was young and on fire. The whole world was ahead of me. I was full of hope and enthusiasm. Although I didn't have tangible plans for my future, I was enjoying life. I was only 22 and I was making things happen. I was working really hard.

First, I went to a beautiful, coastal, vacation town called Ocean City in New Jersey. I was really impressed by how clean, neat, and cosy those small American towns were. *Civilization,* I thought! Immaculately-cut lawns and pretty New England style houses with American flags hanging on them. I lived in a beautiful three-storey Victorian house on Wesley Street. It was known as "Donna's house" because of the landlord's name, and she also lived there.

When the summer season began, the house was packed with students like me who had come from different parts of the world to work in the States. There were about ten bedrooms with three or four beds in each. I found out later that when we thought we were renting a bedroom, we were actually renting a bed or even half of a bed! I ended up sharing one room with five other girls in a 400-square-foot studio with two bunkbeds, two single beds, a cooker, a small kitchen table, a shower, and a toilet. I had to share a bed with another girl.

After about a week, all the initial cuteness and cleanness of the house disappeared. But there was always laughter and fun in our tiny dormitory. Besides, the house was a 5-minute walk from the ocean. And where I came from, luxury could only be viewed on TV anyway. The fact that we lived like kittens in a box didn't bother me at all. I was in America! I could deal with minor inconveniences.

Time usually flies when you are having a great time. And boy, did I have a good time! I was working like a horse (a popular saying in Ukraine), but I did enjoy the ocean, meeting new friends, getting to experience American culture, and of course shopping. However, the program that I came to the USA through was only for the summer period. My flight back home was scheduled for September 17th, 2010. My U.S. visa would end a few days later.

On a deliciously breezy and pleasantly warm evening in August, I was sitting on the porch with a cup of coffee thinking about my life. I had come to America, which had fulfilled my first dream, I had improved my English, I had made good money, and I'd had an incredible life experience. It was time to go back and continue my education, which was such an important priority at the time.

But I was also thinking that I had tasted American life and I hadn't satisfied my hunger yet. I wanted more. I didn't want to go back. I had worked so hard to escape the poverty and hardship there. I decided firmly *not to go back!* As soon as I told myself that, something clicked within me—signifying that it was the right decision. I had learned in life that while making important life decisions, it is crucial to listen to my heart. So I did!

I decided to take the plunge and stay in the land of opportunities. I loved that country. I didn't really care or think about how I was going to make it happen. I was excited and scared. My visa was going to expire in a month. But as Scarlet O'Hara would say, I would think about that the next day! One step at a time.

From ugly duckling to beautiful swan

I didn't have a plan. I didn't know what I was going to do with my life and myself. I didn't have any clarity or awareness. Some people think that if you don't plan for anything great, you won't be disappointed. But guess what, you can still get knocked down even if you don't have a plan. I got knocked down many times. But that's okay. It's all part of the journey that I had to make. I learned that it's okay to be clueless, as long as you aspire for something more significant.

As soon as I overstayed my legal permit, I got fired from one of my restaurant jobs, then I lost the second one, and shortly after, my third job was gone too because the season was over and there were no customers. Ocean City is usually only busy in the summer. I had some savings from my jobs, but they weren't going to last for long. I had to figure out what I was going to do next. I was alone, scared, and clueless. But I had big dreams to keep me alive.

> *Your life is beautiful and precious, and your presence on earth has a unique and graceful purpose.* **I kept reminding myself of this in tough times. Remind yourself of this when you're going through tough times.**

We are all programmed for greatness and outstanding achievements. However, at times we realise our personal beauty and worth the hard way. Sometimes, it is absolutely necessary to hit the bottom before we can climb to the top and celebrate a victory. It is a rollercoaster ride, but reaching the bottom provides a valuable and necessary reference point that makes us grateful for all that we accomplish in life.

> **Remember as you embark on this ride that we all come from a great source no matter what happens. A diamond in the rough is still a diamond.**

When you're at the bottom, it's good to remember the Hans Christian Andersen fairytale about the ugly duckling, which is a powerful and thought-provoking metaphor about transformation and self-discovery.

In the story, there was a duckling who hatched last and looked unusually big and unsightly. After his birth, he was exposed to a great deal of suffering. He was bitten and pushed and taunted. The other ducks pecked him, the chickens beat him, and the girl who fed the poultry kicked him. All the birds in the farmyard disliked and humiliated the poor duckling. Even his mother didn't feel much sympathy for her child. He was different, and everybody saw him as "ugly".

Being alone and miserable, the ugly duckling ran away, frightening the birds in the hedge as he left. A journey full of trials and ordeals had begun. The duckling escaped to a large moor inhabited by wild ducks looking for shelter. They didn't accept him either, only reminding him how ugly he was. Later, he met some geese who mocked him as well. Then he reached a cottage where an old woman, a hen, and a cat lived. But the duckling was different from them too. The poor ugly bird didn't fit in with any community. He was the outcast, alone in his misery, yet he was high in spirit.

The duckling was in search of himself and his purpose, and therefore he was hopeful. One evening, just as the sun set below the radiant clouds, a large flock of beautiful birds appeared. The ugly duckling didn't know who they were, but they seemed majestic to him. They were swans, graceful and shiny, with dazzling whiteness. They uttered a singular cry, spread their glorious wings, and flew away. The duckling felt a weird sensation. During his moment of despair and loneliness, the duckling looked up in the sky and found his inspiration. He was mesmerised by the beauty, grace, and glory of the soaring, magnificent birds. He got a new perspective, a new vision, and a new dream.

Storms and winter passed. The ugly duckling challenged himself to approach the royal birds. He flew up to the graceful swans to meet his death, being sure that he was ugly. He went to them and said, "Kill me!" He bent his head down to the surface of the water and awaited his death. Then, in the water, he saw the reflection of his image—not the ugly and disagreeable duckling—but a graceful and beautiful swan. His catharsis occurred. Through suffering and sorrow, he managed to rise up and shine with glory and majesty.

To some extent, we are all challenged to take the journey of being an ugly duckling who becomes a beautiful swan. I took that journey and I know it's necessary for self-discovery. There are many people who feel "weird" or out of place. They don't belong to a certain circle of friends or don't click with other people despite their intentions. Perhaps you are not walking your true path or are hanging out with the wrong "birds".

> **Our moments of desperation can be truly fascinating.** *Don't ignore them—listen to them.* **During moments of despair, they can bring insights, a better understanding, and a new way of approaching life. Learn to listen to the whispers and you may open your eyes to new horizons. View them as gifts that create growth opportunities—and they will lead to inspiration.**

Perhaps you don't like your job, feel that you don't fit in at your workplace, or aren't generating the results you want. Maybe you're afraid to leave your comfort zone, or you stay in a toxic relationship wrapped up in the false illusion of love. Maybe you lack a sense of reward or satisfaction in your tedious daily routine. These moments of uneasiness—that lead to fear, anger, and resentment—are moments of truth that urge you to discover who you really are.

The tale shows us that the process of evolution isn't always pretty, but it is always rewarding. You need the thrilling and thorny ride of self-discovery with all of its trials, errors, and troubles to completely realise who you really are in this life. Challenge yourself and get ready to uncover the intoxicating glory of your true personality—as you transition from an ugly duckling into a beautiful swan.

The path is sometimes thorny

When you're on the path of self-discovery, the way can often be thorny. Don't let a few thorns stop you! On my way, I often felt like the ugly duckling. I felt out of place in Ukraine—that's why I went to the USA. Then I felt out of place in NJ, working in a restaurant. Although I was meeting new people and making money, I realised that it wasn't for me. Carrying dirty plates wasn't my idea of a dream job.

After the season was over in Ocean City, I decided to test the waters in Miami, Florida. I had heard that it was paradise: a clear, turquoise ocean, white sandy beaches, palm trees, and never-ending summer. And I'd heard that people working in restaurants on the beach were making a fortune. It felt like a great option!

Maybe Miami is paradise to many, but it certainly wasn't paradise for me initially. I faced many challenges looking for a job. It was a struggle. Nobody wanted to hire an illegal immigrant. After weeks of intensive searching, I was happy and relieved to finally get a job. It was a hostess job in one of the restaurants on Ocean Drive, a street right on the beach designed specifically for tourists. I've never seen so many restaurants in such a relatively small area! The street is literally packed with overpriced and poor-quality restaurants, one after the next. I guess "location, location, location" is the only oxygen for those businesses.

My job was to "sit" people who were passing by the restaurant. There were usually tons of people leisurely strolling down the beach enjoying the tropical heat. I was supposed to use all of my charm and social skills to persuade people to dine in the "best place in Miami". (I wouldn't even call it decent, yet alone the best!) To say it was a hard job is an understatement, and it was for minimum wage (a mere $7 per hour).

I was under constant pressure from the manager, the servers, and the busboys. Their pay depended on how many people they served. Sometimes, even the owner stopped by to check how things were going, always giving me that "you've got to work harder" look. And the tourists were sometimes seriously annoyed at being bothered on every single step of their walk, as there was the same system in every restaurant on that street. Despite a huge variety of dining options, they were all very similar in their concept: similar mediocre American food, the same two for one drinks specials, and the same mediocre customer service. It was torture trying to deal with all of that pressure.

I was doing my best trying to sit people, but as I was constantly reminded, it wasn't reflected in the results. The restaurant didn't always look packed. I felt like I was on a survival trial every day. And every day it was the same thing: "Hi! How are you? Would you like to check our menu? We can give you a great deal: two for one drinks! Get the best dining experience on the beach!" "No, thank you" was the usual response, very often with a negative attitude. It was psychologically and physically draining to stand in the sun for eight hours, facing pressure and zero respect from my managers.

Like the ugly duckling, I felt alone and miserable, unappreciated, and humiliated. I started questioning my decision to stay in America. I had burned the bridges of my life in Ukraine by overstaying my visa. But most importantly, I didn't want to go back home like a loser, having achieved nothing.

Of course, my parents would have accepted me back and wouldn't have loved me less for it. I would have had a home and safety, but I would have lost my self-respect. I'd had enough of poverty and limitations, and my soul was aspiring for more, something better. However, that something more seemed a million miles away. In those moments, I really felt the burden of being all by myself in this big world, where nobody gives a monkeys about you. After three months, I quit the job.

Going to America was a big dream for me, and I will always be grateful for it. However, it was so hard at the beginning. Whether we like it or not, nobody is waiting there for us. No one knocked on my door of the tiny studio I was living in and said, "Let me help you young lady. We see a great potential in you." It would be nice, but life doesn't happen that way! You do have unlimited potential within you, but you have to tap it yourself and you have to find your own path in life. *No one will do it for you.*

You have unlimited potential

Many people seem sceptical when they hear the term "unlimited potential". But it is true. We have unlimited potential in the area of our giftedness. I certainly won't ever become a champion in boxing. My body shape isn't suited to life in the ring. But more importantly, boxing is not my area of interest. I am neither good at it, nor am I passionate about it. I know my strengths and *that's* where I have unlimited potential.

The reason why so many people don't live their life to the fullest is because their potential remains untapped. They are not aware of how capable they are; in fact, many people don't even bother to find out what their gifts are. So they stay in jobs they hate, where they don't have even the slightest chance of demonstrating their gifts, creativity, and passion.

> **To live to the fullest, you have to discover where your potential lies. And that comes from identifying your dream.**

Finding my dream

To identify my next dream, I began soul searching. Just like that poor bird, I wasn't successful at the start. I tried different jobs, whatever I could get without professional experience, education, and a legal permit, but I ended up hating them even more than the restaurant jobs, because they weren't bringing in any money. I finally settled at a restaurant called Big Easy, which served New Orleans cuisine in Hollywood, Florida. It was much calmer than Miami, with a relaxed atmosphere, regular local customers, and stable pay. Then I started focusing on how to arrange my legal permit to stay.

I was on a journey of transformation, but without visible effects initially. I wanted to be more; I wanted to have more; I wanted to create more. I was trying to figure out what I wanted to do with my life. I was hungry and searching for something to fulfill me. I knew that great things were coming my way, because those who look for something always find something.

> **Even if you don't see the results, it doesn't mean they aren't there. Don't kill your winner's spirit with impatience. Trust me, the universal forces are always working on your part, even if you aren't consciously aware of it. Change isn't instant. There is a time buffer that keeps the universe from being total chaos. There is no such thing as instantaneous fulfilment of your desires.**

Being an active person who needs to be involved and engaged all the time, I began searching for "something better" in my free time. My curious mind and enormous hunger brought me to different life ventures. I would get hooked on something shiny with big promises, invest some money, trying to buy the "dream life," and then shortly after, I would be disappointed.

I tried multi-level marketing businesses with different companies. The business model is a great opportunity for those who want to create financial independence, but it didn't work for me. If only I had known back then what I know now, I could have become a great success. But I couldn't get the ball rolling because I lacked persistence and tenacity.

Then I tried modelling, something totally different. I listened to the advice of my friends, who would always say, "You have the perfect look for a model. You'll do well." I didn't do well. A couple of castings and fashion gigs helped me understand that I am more than just a pretty face with long legs. That seemingly "glamorous" job seemed shallow and meaningless to me. After that, I learned to filter the advice from others.

> **Unless it is aligned with what you truly want—don't do it.**

Then I decided to go to college. I loved my professors and my learning experience. I signed up for Academic English Writing classes at Broward College, such as composition, rhetoric, creative writing, American Literature, and public speaking. Those courses really helped me improve my English. However, I didn't see great potential there, apart from getting in debt. I didn't feel that they would give me the tools to practically apply the knowledge I was learning. And to get a degree, I had to take a lot of what seemed like unnecessary classes. So, I didn't last more than three semesters there.

Then I started reading books and going to seminars, workshops, and conferences in the area of personal growth and development. When I was at the live event, exposing myself to the transformation and empowerment and expanding my mind—all of a sudden, it hit me—"I want to be a motivational speaker!" As soon as I got that thought, it felt right in my mind and it felt good in my heart. I knew that I had discovered my sweet spot. As I thought about it more, I realised that dream, that gift, had been within me my entire life.

I remembered back in Ukraine, one of the first books I read was a translation of Dale Carnegie's book on public speaking. I absolutely loved the content and back then, I thought how amazing it would be for me to be able to speak with such confidence and ease one day, like it was described in the books.

It was a dream-fantasy, and it was inspiring, but it was very far-fetched from the reality I was living in. To my knowledge, there were no motivational speakers in Ukraine at the time. So…I forgot about it.

When I attended that live event in Florida, I was impressed by the speakers on stage, who looked and behaved in such a graceful way, sharing their wisdom, and inspiring the masses to take charge of their lives. I felt I could do the same. I had an incredible story to share, with lots of struggles, but a lot of accomplishments too. Maybe I hadn't given myself enough credit for them, but I had achieved a lot. I thought *I could do this as well.*

> **An idea doesn't come to you unless you are already resourced and gifted at it to bring it to life and to make it successful. It is useful to remember this when you are trying to get clarity on your dream.**

So, I got a new dream: becoming a professional speaker. It felt good! But how would I do it? I didn't know. That dream was a million miles away from me. I continued working at the restaurant. One night, I was serving a party of rich people who were laughing, sharing stories, having a good time, and enjoying life. I was thinking, *What am I doing here, serving these beautiful people? I should be among them!*

I thought, *I am in the USA, in the land of opportunities, yet I am working just as hard as I was in Ukraine, in the land of no opportunities.*

Something was off. I looked at my coworker Rosemary, who was born in America. She worked just as hard as me, and she had nothing, the same as me.

Then it hit me: it's not enough to just be *around* opportunities in order to benefit from them. You have to be able to see them and *seize them*. And that requires **stepping up, taking risks, exiting the comfort zone,** and **doing things you're afraid of.** With all respect to Rosemary, as she was a lovely girl, I didn't want to end up like her. I had a dream of becoming a professional motivational speaker. So I stepped up from being a server in a restaurant to become a server of the world.

That was the cathartic moment of revelation to me, my transformation into the swan. Nothing noticeably changed outside for me, but everything changed on the inside. There is so much power behind the expression: **your inner world creates your outer world.** That was the case for me, when I harnessed my dream with a confident decision. I realised that a life transition happens not when you move to a different country, but when something changes within.

> **You might have heard that change is a different way of doing. Well, transformation is a different way of being. I felt that I began my transformation. I stopped calling myself a server and started thinking of myself as a speaker.**

How to identify your dream

Some people already have a dream life in mind. But if you don't, it's time to find it. My dream was going to America, and then becoming a motivational speaker. However, you don't need to change your place of residence or your country, like I did. "You need to align with yourself and your aspirations, and discover your true desires.

> **To do this, you need to begin with self-awareness. You need to know yourself, what your strengths are, and what your interests are.**

This may involve your career, vocation, or job. In these cases, your dream has to be in the middle of **your strengths and your area of interests.** It has to fill your soul with joy. It has to be something you're gifted in, because you'll have unlimited potential in this area. You have to do what reflects you as a person, and what the representation is of your higher version of yourself.

> **Ask yourself questions, like:**
> - What inspires me most of all?
> - What brings joy to my life?
> - What would I like my life to look like?
> - What would my ideal day be like?
> - When was the last time I lost track of time because I was so immersed in doing something?
> - What am I good at?
> - Where does my heart lie?
> - What would I be willing to do if I wasn't getting paid?
> - Where is my hunger?

Your dream needs to be meaningful, with substance. It must be the extension of you that can never be taken away from you. You have to do this yourself. Nobody is going to do it for you. Don't sit there and wait to be discovered or to get lucky. It isn't going to happen. If you haven't found your life purpose, your dream, keep looking, keep searching, keep asking questions. But never settle for mediocrity.

If you place value outside of yourself—your possessions, your business, you are in a big trouble. All those things can be taken away from you: they can be broken, destroyed, stolen. And when all of those seemingly great outside things are gone, you are left with nothing.

It amazes me how many people place price tags on their source of fulfilment. "If I had a bigger house, a better car, a bigger bank account, I would be happy." But that's not the case. These people are living an illusion. I love luxurious things, as they add colour to our life, *but they don't create meaning*. Meanings are in people, feelings, and moments, but not things.

I'm not saying it's not about money. Possessions and beautiful things make our life easier and more attractive. But they can never fill the void in our soul. True meaning lies much deeper than money can reach. It lies in our awareness of who we are and the difference we are making in our lives and the lives of others. Any material blessings are side effects of our goals; they come along when we reach our goals and life aspirations.

If you ask any successful person what their goals are, most won't say "money". Money is something that accompanied the realisation of their goals. Money and material possessions can be taken away from you, but your personal value will remain untouched, because it is inside you. You have the total power to control it. And it comes from being aware of who you are.

Do what you love

A few years back, I visited San Diego zoo and it was an outstanding experience! There is always something special about nature and animals that gives me tons of positive energy.

One of the best parts of the day was the "zoo man," a guy who gave us an exciting, one of a kind tour of the zoo. His passion and enthusiasm toward animals was incredible and awe-inspiring. As soon as we embarked on the bus, he started impersonating the animals with great skill. He joked and told stories about the various residents of the zoo, referring to their unique personalities. He knew every animal by name. The level of devotion to his profession was impressive!

Everyone on the bus was having a blast, constantly laughing, and clapping. The energy around him was brimming with vitality, passion, and power. He was truly a happy man, absolutely enjoying his life. His energy, which was full of life and enthusiasm, stirred my soul. It was such a powerful message that defines everything in life: success, achievement, fulfilment, and happiness. The message is simple, yet so profound:

> **Love what you do. Do what you love.**

How many people enjoy what they are doing? I mean really enjoy their occupation? How many go to work—not because it pays their bills, but because of a deeper meaning singing to their soul and mind?

It is a blessing when your occupation merges with your life's passion. However, it is not a lucky set of circumstances when your profession reflects your heart's desires and aspirations. Finding a career that reflects your heart's aspirations is the result of **focus, determination, self-discipline, and hard work.** You need to take action and put in the effort.

However, find a way to turn your hobby into a profitable occupation and it won't feel like work. Finding the right career for you will be different for everyone, and it's why you have to know what you love doing. Don't just accept the job you were told to do because it's considered "normal" or because people told you that it's all you could do.

Think about back when you were a child, when you wanted to do or create something before people said you couldn't. It is a challenging but rewarding experience when you have the courage to follow your dreams. If you love what you are doing, it is true happiness. Life becomes fascinating when you are doing what you love.

"Let the beauty of what you love be the beauty of what you do." –
Rumi

> **Your occupation needs to reflect your interests.**
> **So what are they?**
> **What if you wanted to write a book or start a business?**
> **What if you always wanted to start a non-profit organization to help kids?**

Be success first

When you know your dream, then it's time to start making it happen. But in our busy, hectic world, we often forget about our true nature. We are human **be**ings. So before you do anything, you have to *be* something. **You are, then you do, and then you have.** This sequence needs to be observed if you want to live harmoniously.

Your self-image, how you think about and see yourself, comes first—before you decide to take any action. And your self-image affects every result that you get. The way you become successful is that first, you are success and then you become successful. **Who are you in your life?** How aware are you about yourself and your life?

When I declared "I am a speaker," everything around me changed, because my self-image changed. My life acquired a whole new meaning.

> There is enormous power behind the words "I am". When you tell yourself "I am a writer, a singer, a dancer, a gardener, an artist, a pianist, a stylist, a designer, a hair dresser, a realtor, a sales representative, a speaker; I am a leader, I am a creator, I am powerful, I am confident, I am creative, I am awesome, I am intentional, I am resourceful, I am a magnet for all I aspire for", you begin manifesting your reality. You can be whoever you want to be. Become the active creator of your life.

"Success is not to be pursued; it is attracted by the person you become."
– **Jim Rohn**

The stages of passion

I have heard so many times that you need to be passionate about your dream. Yes, passion is important. However, nowadays, the term "passion" is overused to the point that it doesn't carry the meaning that it's meant to. "Passion" means having a burning desire within that wakes you up in the morning, helps you stay motivated, and keeps your eyes on your vision. However, it doesn't mean having all-or-nothing thinking. If something doesn't go to plan, you adjust your actions and behaviours. It has its high and low seasons.

In my own life experience, I realised that passion has its own seasons. In the beginning, my passion was about **hunger.** I was hungry for knowledge, for the right connections, the right opportunities. And many times, that hunger-passion was infused with frustration and a lack of the desired results despite my actions. I was impatient and hungry, kind of like a child who sees a toy but cannot get it yet!

Then my passion led me to **curiosity.** I became more calm and relaxed. I gained the wisdom to value the law of the process—that my dream cannot be achieved overnight. This was an eye-opening shift for me. I started looking more within, being curious about myself, and my life, and my place in it.

At this stage, I realised that the answer is always *within you.* When you combine this self-knowledge with your personal resourcefulness, you become an unstoppable force. It became clear to me then that we don't get what we want—we get *who we are.* So, I started living my empowering principles and beliefs in life's greatness, acting in a way that was in accordance with them. For this reason, I firmly believe that the curiosity stage of passion carries the most potential.

When I began looking inside, I started receiving invitations to speak at different events I applied for, whereas before I was unsuccessful. I knew it was the result of me embracing the truth that success is attracted to the person you are. In my actions, I was now attracting the right events and people, because I had self-knowledge and inner resourcefulness.

> **The more you look deep within you, the more you develop your thinking and your character, and the more effective you become in your actions. Curious, searching questions can help you understand your purpose and find your dream. They can also help you on the journey of your dreams.**

Always ask questions! Focused questions have the ability to unlock your creativity and imagination. Learn the fifty shades of your personality. Be inquisitive, be curious! Your own reality is the projection of your consciousness level. Your mind will see what it is capable to see, what it is trained to see. To create great things, such as your dream life, you need to be able to see great things, and to see great things you need to be a person who is able to see the possibility of great things.

It's important to avoid all-or-nothing thinking here. Passion has different faces, and it has its high and slow seasons. High or low, it should always be aligned with your heart's longings. Even in the low seasons, you must be *curious*. There is less stress, more thinking, and more understanding in curiosity than with hunger. Start with curiosity. Get on the move, then develop the momentum, and see what happens. Curiosity lets you start small and build big. It is a powerful emotion that can give rise to something magnificent in your life. What are you curious about?

The final stage of passion is about **fulfilment.** This is the stage when your imagination merges with your reality, when you get to reap the fruits of your labour, when you see the results of your efforts. And it is the stage of maturity. You realise that happiness and success are not the final station you will arrive at—they are the manner of travelling.

When you accomplish one goal, it's not the final destination. There will be another bigger and more demanding goal. But the good news is that the higher you go, the more capable you become, and the easier it becomes for you to tackle the challenges that come with reaching for new and exciting goals.

I'm happy to say that I am absolutely passionate about what I do in life: inspirational speaking, writing, travelling the world for work and pleasure, and often combing the two, and doing these things bring me absolute joy. My passion has different faces.

Hunger-Curiosity-Fulfillment

Summary

If you don't know where you are going, how do you expect to get there? Many people struggle because they want a better life, but they have no idea what a better life looks like for them. Your dreams bring clarity and direction in your life. To find your dreams, you have got to go through the journey of gaining self-awareness, understanding who you are, what your strengths and weaknesses are, what you are capable of, where your passions lie, and what you would love to do. Awaken your curiosity and ask yourself self-searching questions. You need to do what you love, what brings you joy, and what brings you closer to enjoying your dream life.

If you haven't found what your dream looks like yet, keep searching, stay hungry, ask questions, take chances, until you find what truly resonates with your heart. It's never too late. If you already know your purpose and your dream, but you don't know how to bring it to fruition, then keep reading, as we'll look at this in the rest of the book.

Every day offers a new insight, a new perspective, and a new opportunity. Never settle for less, because you know that you can have more. If your mind came up with a certain idea, you have the power to make it happen. Listen to your heart, believe in yourself, grasp the opportunity, and take action. Don't think too much; the universe doesn't wait. Life is yours! You are the creator of your life.

CHAPTER 4

Only You Can Make Your Dream Life a Reality

"Cherish your visions and dreams as they are the children of your soul; blueprints of your ultimate achievements." – **Napoleon Hill**

Over the course of my life, I have discovered that **you are the only person who can bring your dream to life.** Nobody can do it for you. Regardless of your present conditions and circumstances, you hold the power to choose a new direction for your life. Your past and present do not have to define your future. Each day, you get a chance to start anew, with new energy, new thoughts and ideas, and new actions.

Of course, there is a period of getting your feet wet. However, you absolutely *must* start taking actions to change your life before you think you are ready, before you have everything figured out, before you have the answers to all the "how's, what's, and where's." All you've got to do is take one step at a time, putting one foot in front of the other, building momentum, and always doing the best you can. Take responsibility for making your life better.

Stop the excuses

Many people are used to complaining or blaming outside circumstances for their misfortune. It might be their job, the economy, self-serving politicians, the environment they are in, the lack of resources, the lack of time, or anything else standing in the way of them living a fulfilled life.

But in fact, none of those circumstances have anything to do with the quality of your life. Life neither favours you nor dislikes you. It is neutral. It treats you just like everyone else. If you don't like your current surroundings, **you can change them** by following your dream and your heart. However, instead of cultivating a compelling vision of their dream life, people create excuses.

By constructing these excuses and believing in them (and what you believe in becomes your reality), people delegate their power to outside forces. Therefore, their life remains at the mercy of random circumstances. Or in other words, *they* remain stuck in the life they have now, rather than trying to get the life they want.

For these people, it's much easier to blame the outside world rather than assume responsibility and start living intentionally. But is it *really* easier in the long run? If you have no dream to follow, no plan to accomplish, you end up just going with the flow and living at the mercy of whatever happens to you externally. So in the long term, it's not easier, because you don't live your dream life.

Dr. Wayne Dyer wisely observed, *"If you think other people are the cause of your problem, you are going to need to send the rest of the world to a psychiatrist for you to get better."*

Take responsibility

The majority of people I interact with ask me, "I know what I want in life, but HOW can I achieve it?" Before anything else, you must assume 100% responsibility for your life. You need to understand that every single result has been created by you, consciously or unconsciously. It might be hard to accept this, but a cause and effect relationship is always present in life.

Cause is always you—your thoughts, your words, your actions, your energy, and your behaviour. Assuming responsibility for your life empowers you, because you develop your conscious ability to respond to life's challenges. Hence the word "ResponseAbility" (the *ability to respond* to life consciously, not react unconsciously). The sooner you accept total responsibility over your life, the sooner you can start building your dream!

> **You have the power to change your life by taking responsibility for your life. This doesn't mean you have to blame yourself for your previous mistakes and errors. It means evaluating your present reality and asking yourself "What have I done to find myself in this reality?" By staying with the question, you see how your actions and behaviour, or your thinking and your energy have caused your current experience.**

By doing this, you start to understand the law of cause and effect that governs the universe—and a major transformation happens within you. You stop blaming and complaining about your circumstances, and you start to see your role in them. After all, how can you blame the universe if you step into traffic and get hit by a car?

Likewise, it also means not playing the victim to your circumstances. Everyone faces challenges and difficult times, but it's how you respond to them that matters. Whatever your circumstances in life, whatever your background, you can take responsibility for how you react to it, for what you do next, for how you treat yourself, and for how you change your circumstances.

If you're standing on the pavement and you get hit by a drunk driver who loses control of their car, you didn't create those circumstances, but you can create your response to them. You can choose to be bitter and angry at the world for what happened to you, and nothing will get better, or you can choose to respond positively, to overcome your situation, and to be loving. Your circumstances don't define you and what your life will be.

By assuming responsibility for everything you have, you can start thinking what you need to do differently in order to get what you'd like to have.

Do it before you are ready

When you've taken responsibility for your life, then you need to start living it and doing what it takes to make life better. One of my great mentors Paul Martinelli said, "You are going to learn how to fly when you are in the air, not in the nest. You have to jump and build your wings on the fly".

This was a great encouragement for me, because I didn't feel like I was ready to actively pursue my dream of becoming a speaker. I had a lot of limitations regarding my skills and capabilities. The fact that English wasn't my native language was a psychological burden for me. I was thinking, "Who would want to listen to me and what I have to say with my broken English and my heavy accent?" But I still started taking action, doing things I was afraid of, and jumping with the hope of building my wings on the fly.

Action builds the foundation to your dream—it gives the oxygen to it. Start acting before you think you are ready.

The law of diminishing intent says, "The longer you wait to do something you should do now, the greater the odds that you will never actually do it."

What I've learnt is that somehow there is never a perfect time and a perfect stage of readiness. I've noticed that some people are always getting ready, and never accomplishing anything. You just have to take that leap and do it now.

"If you can't fly then run, if you can't run then walk, if you can't walk then crawl, but whatever you do you have to keep moving forward." –
M. L. King

That's what I did. I started taking massive action. And let me tell you, there were many times when I was moving in the wrong direction. And frankly, there were a lot of times when I had no idea what I was doing, and I was frustrated thinking it was a waste of time.

> But there is never "a waste". There is not one "right" way to your dream; there are multiple ways. And each step you take—you need to take, because it prepares you to enter the next, grander version of your life. Once you start working on your dream, eventually your dream starts working on you. As a result, you grow and develop, and walk gracefully into your life's purpose.

Work on your dream

People love the *idea* of a dream, but they don't love the idea of working on the dream, especially if there isn't enough clarity, or when things initially go wrong. We all are fired up at the beginning, but when we don't see results right away, we lose our excitement, and we quit. Don't let that happen to you.

I realised that you can't make your dream happen by simply wishing and wanting. As Les Brown says, *"Wishing and wanting is never enough. If that was the case, everyone would be skinny, rich, and happy."*

I knew I needed to work on my dream, so I joined the toastmasters club to develop my speaking skills (a global non-profit educational organization that helps people develop communication and public speaking skills). When I went to my first meeting, I was impressed with the atmosphere, and I was lucky to attend on a night of invited guest speakers.

After listening to my reason for coming to toastmasters, the president of the club, Sheila, said to me with a broad smile, "Anna, you are in the right place. You will see how far you can go." I was hooked and thrilled. The guest speakers were great, confident, articulate, and inspiring. It was like they turned up the atmosphere in the room.

After the speeches finished, there was a "table topics" section of the meeting, when all the members and guests could participate in impromptu speech on a given topic for a few minutes. I raised my hand to see how I fitted in the community and to test the waters. I was ready to jump into this thing too, and build my wings on the way down. I was excited when I was sitting in my chair, but as soon as I got up, all of my excitement was substituted with fear.

As George Jessel wisely observed, *"The mind is a wonderful thing. It starts working the minute you are born and never stops until you get up to speak in public."*

I was assigned to speak on the fear of public speaking. I couldn't believe how relevant the topic was to my emotional state. I was petrified. Life can sure be ironic. I had no idea what I was saying, but I remember going as fast as I could just to get it over with. I was happy and miserable when I finished: happy because I had got through it, and miserable because I did a terrible job. My first speaking experience in the USA was a total disaster, and I felt like a total failure.

> **When you try something for the first time, no matter how passionate you are about it, you are going to fail. When you discover your gift, it's presented to you in the form of a piece of rock. It's up to you whether you want to turn it into a diamond with your consistent efforts, hard work, and a lot of pressure.**

What I came to realise is that sometimes, failure is more important than success. Because if you are serious about your dream, then failure can be a powerful stimulator for your growth. As a result, you push your own limits, you set higher expectations for yourself, and you go that extra mile. The majority of us wish to have an extraordinary life. But most people begin with ordinary. How do you turn an ordinary life into an extraordinary one? By doing something **extra:** extra action, extra effort, extra you.

After the first meeting, I was frustrated, but I didn't get discouraged. I signed up for membership of Toastmasters and started attending every meeting, preparing, and presenting speeches every two weeks. I was in hot pursuit of my dream. My speeches weren't any good though (in case you're wondering). They were completely rubbish. But that wasn't the point. I was smart enough (which doesn't happen often) to understand that my dream was too big to fit my current reality, therefore I was on the mission to grow myself to fit into that dream—by getting good. Really good!

At the same time, I tried holding various workshops in an attempt to share my knowledge in the area of personal development, to practice my public speaking skills, and to inspire people to take control of their lives. This was even when I had no idea what I was doing! I invited my friends who were sceptical about the empowering ideas I was banging on about. Out of respect for me, they would come and support me. They weren't going to take any action afterwards and frankly, I wasn't sure whether they were even listening to my "seminars".

Those were my first pitiful attempts at public speaking besides Toastmasters, with four or five people there at most. I had the feeling that I was running a fool's errand. But I was taking action. I was moving towards my dreams. I had my eyes fixed on the goal. I was creating momentum.

Watching the recordings of my first speeches makes me cringe now. But at the same time, the recognition awards and trophies I got for winning toastmasters speech contests bring a broad smile to my face and make me proud when I look at them now. We are so attracted to words like "genius," "talent," "gift," and "charisma," thinking they serve as the key to life's greatness—but the key is in **taking action.**

No effort and no action go unnoticed. Every action matters in the big picture—as long as you are intentional about your steps. Do it when you are afraid, do it before you are ready, do it now!

Dealing with perfection

Some people don't start working on their dream because they think their dream has to be perfect. Most people think about a "life purpose" as something that needs to be world-changing and huge, and nothing less than excellence will do it justice. However, this couldn't be further from the truth.

Unfortunately, this illusion of perfection and needing to be "the best" stops people from taking action. All-or-nothing thinking is a proven way to accept mediocrity in life. People try to compare themselves to their ideals. But it's like a horizon—you can never achieve it. Therefore, you remain bound.

> **Instead of focusing on the huge gap between your current reality and your ideal one, which puts you in a low emotional state, focus on measuring backwards. Give yourself credit for what you have achieved already.**

My husband always says, "We all are perfect, we are just not consciously aware of our perfection…the divinity we are." But so many people remain oblivious to their amazing inner selves and self-knowledge because they are conditioned to measure their worthiness based on their achievements and possessions. Most of the time, people go through life never discovering their gifts and talents. But we all possess a great deal of greatness; it is just a matter of discovering it through giving life to our gifts.

We are perfect as human beings. If you doubt that you are perfect, try thinking of how pure you were as a pure child. But just because we are perfect, this doesn't mean that we have to do everything perfectly. This means don't be afraid to mess things up, to make mistakes, and to grow because of them.

Have high standards for yourself and your life, but don't wait around for the perfect moment with the perfect circumstances, as you might turn down opportunities or even be unable to see them.

You don't need to be great to start. But you have to start to be great. If you allow the unglamorous process of doing to come to your service and you do the work, then you will discover a lot of life's treasures. Trust yourself. You know more than you think you do. You come from the all-powerful creative source of the universe. You were created out of greatness to live a life of greatness.

Do your best where you are

You might not be where you aspire to be now, but you are where you are, so your job is to get the best out of it. While I was aspiring to be a motivational speaker, I was still working as a waitress. Waitressing wasn't for me, and I hated serving. Carrying trays and dirty plates, serving rude customers, and having a happy smile on my face when I wanted to cry wasn't my idea of the American Dream.

However, it was my only source of income, so I had to suck it up and do it while pursuing my dream. Although it was emptying my soul, waitressing was paying my bills.

All that time, I knew that I had brilliance within me and that I was capable of being, doing, and having more. It was a miserable and beautiful place to be in. The distance between my real self and my ideal self, seemed like a million miles away.

> **What do you do when you aren't satisfied with your life, yourself, your job, and your results? You do your best. Even in the job you hate, especially in the job you hate. The skills you acquire in the job that makes you sick will serve you in the dream that elevates your soul.**

I was where I was. And I was trying to get the best out of it. I was doing my best serving people, working on my English, and developing a hard work ethic. I was creating enthusiastic energy around me that made my detestable job not that detestable.

At some point, it stopped being about my job and started being about my personality and myself. It's never about the job anyway—it's always about you, your personality, and your skill set. By working, you don't serve your employer—you serve you.

I used to say that waitressing paid my bills, but I was wrong. It wasn't waitressing that paid my bills—it was me! I put my efforts, energy, skills, and myself in that job. There was a major shift for me, because I realised that there is no potential in outside resources, such as your job, the economy, and opportunities. **The potential is inside you,** and there is always potential in you.

> **Engaging fully in the seemingly unimportant steps will help you engage fully in the defining moments of your life—when the opportunity knocks. Because how you show up for anything determines how you show up for everything.**

How you perform at any given stage of your life will determine how far you are going to go. So rather than wishing you weren't where you are now, realise that you need every step on the staircase of your life. You can't take the elevator to success; you can't skip stairs either.

My waitressing experience prepared me to gracefully enter the grander version of my life and myself. I realised that every step I had to take, even the unpleasant ones, brought me to where I am today. What I've learned is that you have to dream big, but be good at where you are too.

> **By developing the habit of being and doing your best, you become intentional in thinking on the front end. You begin to comprehend that there are no insignificant moments. Every moment counts, and there is always something going on. Life is in session now.** *Are you present? Are you doing your best?*

Be your best, forget the rest

What if you don't believe that your "best" is good enough? What if you unconsciously fall into the comparison trap—comparing yourself to other people? The answer is: **do not ever compare yourself to anybody!**

This is a lesson I learned when I visited one of the most luxurious resorts in Florida, called The Breakers. It's a beautiful place, with the opulent style of a Renaissance castle, where luxury meets exquisite art. It feels almost royal. When I was there, I felt wonderful. However, I knew I wasn't at the same level as most of the people there.

When I was talking to someone, we touched on the subject of travelling. He made an arrogant little remark, "Oh, I don't fly commercial airlines. I have my own private jet." I thought the comment was arrogant, but he didn't mean it this way—he was speaking from his reality.

As a person who doesn't have a private jet yet, unconsciously I started comparing myself to his success, and it didn't feel great. We tend to compare other people's strengths to our weaknesses. The way he spoke, it sounded so easy and effortless to be successful that I thought "Wow! Why it couldn't be so easy in my life?"

I hadn't even bothered to consider the struggles and obstacles that he had overcome. Every successful person encounters challenges and struggles—that's how achievement in life works. Just look at Oprah Winfrey's life if you want an example. She was born and raised in poverty, and had a difficult upbringing, but she managed to become the first black female billionaire. Everyone faces their own challenges.

I didn't consider that this guy was in his late sixties and may have lived a life of challenges before that. I was just impressed by his present results. Usually, when we look at someone who is successful, we see them as inspiration, as the top of the mountain, but we don't think about the process of climbing that mountain, which is about perspiration. In fact, we often forget that there is always a mountain.

"Genius is one percent inspiration and 99 percent perspiration." – **Thomas Edison**

Looking at those people with their Rolex, or Cartier, Rolls Royce, or Bentley, I suddenly realised that I was depriving myself of my own power. Because my attention was directed to other people's lives and successes, and not my own life and my own success.

> **When we compare ourselves to those who we feel are superior, we feel inferior. When we compare ourselves to those who are inferior, we feel superior. When we stop comparing ourselves to others, we concentrate on our own power.**

Get inspired by others, model their patterns of thinking and behaviour, adopt their strategies, but **always focus on yourself.** Have clear goals, work hard, have patience, be positive, and aim yourself toward success no matter what. That is the fastest and shortest way to life fulfilment.

You have to do your best from the place in your life where you currently are. In one way or another, we take the journey from bad to good to best. But your best yesterday isn't as good as your best today. That's the beauty of growth. As you grow, you have to appreciate the value of the process. Your potential is unlimited if you are operating in your strength zone, i.e from where you are strongest.

It's easier when you take one step at a time. It's like climbing a mountain—it's hard and challenging, but it is so worth it to enjoy the view. You've got to get out there and start climbing, which means **taking action.**

Dreams don't work unless we do

I love inspirational stories, books, and movies that keep the quest for adventure burning strong in my soul. But on their own, they are useless. One of my favourites is *The Secret*. When I first watched it, I experienced an intoxicating exhilaration that pumped me up for quite a while, because it made realising hopes and dreams look like a breeze. I expected my own immediate success story; however, nothing happened. Then I became frustrated and disappointed. I understood and embraced all of the ideas, but there were no changes.

In all my euphoria, I forgot that dreams only turn into reality with **focused action.**

You need to decide what that looks like for you. It might not seem clear to you right now, but don't be discouraged. As long as you are moving, everything will fall into place. Once you find out what inspires your heart and brings a smile to your face, remember that taking action is the catalyst that will crystallise those dreams into reality!

> **Whether it's taking a class to increase your expertise, taking a public speaking course to gain more confidence, learning a foreign language, hiring a coach to help you transform your negative beliefs, going more to networking events to get more clients, adopting a new marketing strategy to increase your business, or signing up for a dating website... Whatever areas in your life you're not happy with, you have to do something about them.**

You have personal power. Merge it with the power of the universe and it will help you reach your own summit!

Summary

Remember, it is you who holds the power over your life. It is you who can make your dream a reality. Any change or transformation begins with taking responsibility for your life and your results. Remember that dreams don't work unless you do, so start taking action—and start before you think you are ready. Don't wait for the perfect time or the perfect moment. Don't try to be perfect, because it's like trying to reach the horizon. Aim to be remarkable instead, by bringing your uniqueness or your gifts to the world.

CHAPTER 5
Find the Meaning of Your Life

"If I have the choice over my life, I choose to live each day with joy, happiness, gratitude, love, and wonder." – **Anna Simpson**

My meaning of life is simple: "Life is beautiful—down to the smallest detail". What is yours? If we formulate our own meaning of life based on a positive foundation, we get to fully enjoy all of our experiences. Then, even difficulties are perceived from a positive perspective, and they will be transformed into learning lessons and new possibilities. Indeed, there is beauty in the challenges, as they are always followed by opportunities.

If you doubt that life is beautiful, you don't need to go far to appreciate life's beauty. Simply open your eyes and heart to the majesty of the universe: from the infinite sky to the powerful ocean, the mesmerising sunrise, the exciting thunderstorms, the salty breeze, the chirping birds, and the magnificent mountains; from a genuine child's smile to the pensive wise look of an elder. There is beauty and inspiration around every corner. Life is beautiful; it is so simple, yet so powerful. When we have positive expectations of life, the universe will respond accordingly.

In this chapter, we'll look at how you can discover and create meaning in your life, live life with fulfilment, be the very best you can using your passion, and live a life of significance.

Life opens up when we do…

Your personal meaning of life shapes your destiny because it creates your thoughts, actions, and results. So, make sure the way you define life inspires your soul to become a creator. For example, the definition "Life is an achievement" will create a much different experience from the definition "Life is a struggle". The mentality "Every cloud has a silver lining" changes everything, and it becomes easier to make the best of the way things turn out.

My belief that "life is beautiful" is not just the romantic perception of a naive soul. It is a deep and well-thought-out philosophy of life. I'll explain: we all love and enjoy the beauty in obvious things. But there is a problem here, and it is that these things only give us fleeting moments of pleasure. The "sparkles" quickly wear off. How long are you excited about your new car? Maybe until it gets the first dent?

I trained myself to see the beauty beyond the obvious things. It's more fun. It's the application of the "the treasure in the trash" principle. One of the biggest secrets in life is that if there is no pain, there is no pleasure to gain. I see beauty in my mistakes and failures, as I'm learning and growing. I see beauty in difficulties and challenges, as they test my mental toughness. I see beauty when I'm down, as I work on my resilience and discover something new about myself. I see beauty when I'm in a bad mood, as I appreciate positive moments more when they finally return.

Whatever happens, there is always a new chance, a fresh perspective, an empowering possibility. Knowing that life is beautiful makes the tough moments easier. It gives me power to keep going despite difficulties. Isn't the thunderstorm storm beautiful, rather than dark and scary? It might sound clichéd, but I love this expression—*our task is not to pray for the storm to pass; we have to learn to dance in the rain.* That's the beauty of life!

"Anyone who has never made a mistake has never tried anything new."
– Albert Einstein

What's wrong in life is always evident—and so is what's right. It's up to us what to select as our focus, and that focus determines the way we feel and experience all that comes our way. Whatever our mission in life, we all aspire for fulfilment. Fulfilment is when we say "Life is beautiful"—and we really mean it. Because we see beauty in every step. We appreciate life not just for its great moments, but in itself—with the good and the bad.

It's a similar feeling to emerging yourself in the cool ocean on a hot summer's day—you feel a blissful pleasure. Or when you finally accomplish the project you've been working on for months. Or when someone you deeply care about says "I love you", which elevates your heart to enormous heights. The only difference is that fulfilment lasts longer.

Fulfilment is when you feel alive—as a fully-fledged soaring personality. However, fulfilment isn't about reaching the final destination; it's about how you travel toward it. Ultimately, life fulfilment comes from the way you view your life experiences. Instead of saying "I failed", try saying "I now know which ways don't work." By doing this, you'll create a difference in energy flow, which will pave the way to your desirable achievement, and consequently will bring the greatest fulfilment.

Life opens up for those who give it inspiring meaning. When you say "It's great!" you invite the greatness. It's the same when you say "Don't think of the pink elephant!" or "Don't look for the colour blue!" The very act of mentioning something brings attention to it. We all have this power, but few of us use it.

"Life is beautiful!" Keep saying it like you mean it. Fake it until you make it. Trust me, it does work! To me, life is beautiful because I'm doing what I'm truly passionate about: inspiring people by reminding them of their enormous power and unlimited potential, encouraging them to believe in themselves and go after their dreams. I inspire them to become leaders of their lives, to create the life they dream about, to live with passion and fulfilment. Isn't it beautiful? It is my humble attempt to make the world a better place.

"Sharks are born knowing they are predators. Sheep understand they are prey. Humans are the only creatures on earth given the choice." –
Unknown

Maybe it's your kids and family who fulfil your heart, or helping other people, or some accomplishments you're proud of. You get to choose what life means to you. As I have previously mentioned and it's important to reiterate it, "there is no universal meaning to things. There is only the meaning you give it." When you have an inspiring definition of life, it's easier to stay in your creative zone. Every step and every endeavour becomes smoother. Once you have a positive and inspiring outlook on life, your dreams and aspirations come to you easier.

If you doubt this, remember where I told you I began in life. By changing my perspective, I changed my life. As I'm writing this, I'm sitting on the balcony of a stunning three-story villa in Marco Island, Florida, with an overview of the spectacular Gulf of Mexico. It's so quiet and peaceful here, a mesmerising and inspiring place with still turquoise waters, white sandy beaches, pensive palm trees, chirping crickets, warbling tropical birds, and a pleasant ocean breeze—my version of paradise on earth.

It's the perfect atmosphere to relax, recharge my energy, and get my creative juices flowing. I'm indulging my senses with overflowing joy. I smile thinking that if someone told me six years ago that I would be vacationing in such a spectacular luxurious place, I would never believe them.

It's funny how life transforms itself almost in a miraculous way when you transform yourself from the inside. I am grateful, blessed, and happy. I understand that my reality began shifting for me once my mind started shifting more toward the bright and beautiful colours of life, toward positive things, toward "possibility thinking".

> **Once our dreams are welcomed by our positive energy, they become part of our reality sooner. To dream, to love, to pursue our aspirations, to live with passion becomes an enjoyable journey when we have an inspiring definition of life. When you go to life with open arms, it opens up in return.**

The footprints we leave behind

As I look at the beautiful sandy beach, I notice some footprints, and I think about the footprints I'll leave behind—my legacy. We all have the opportunity to leave a positive impression in the world, to leave our footprints in the sand.

To create a compelling meaning of your life, you need to think about the legacy you are going to create. It starts with the questions: Why my presence on this earth is important? What difference does my life make?

The secret I've learned is that when I begin with the end in mind, my life acquires more meaning. So now, I'll tell you a story that got me thinking about the importance of legacy.

"Would you like to come to England?" The question came from a person who within a short period of time had left a significant footprint in my life, and who is now my husband. "For a week or two, just a visit for now," he said. "You'll love this beautiful land."

I was hooked! I love travelling and exploring new places, and I had never been to England before. I am a person of adventure! I'm not afraid to take risks and boldly approach life; I moved alone from Ukraine to the United States at 21—and that required a lot of courage.

We landed at Heathrow Airport in London on a grey and rainy day. Coming from hot and sunny Miami, cold and rainy London was quite a contrast. Nonetheless, I was excited and ready to explore. As we left the busy airport, we headed to Worcestershire County, and I was introduced to the lavish green countryside of this wonderful country.

Create The Life You Dream About

We stayed in Hanley Castle in the Malvern Hills—a cosy, peaceful, and serene paradise surrounded by miles of pristine nature. It was an idyllic place to relax, reflect upon life, communicate with nature, and reconnect with the source of our creativity. In such moments of introspection, I realise that life and the world have so much to offer. Every morning there, I woke up feeling grateful.

I grew up in a small village in Ukraine, and as you might imagine, Ukrainian villages are very different from English ones. Even though there was a stark contrast, I could remember my childhood and relate it to the quiet and peaceful atmosphere I was experiencing—the chirping of birds, the delightful fragrances of flowers and blossoming trees, and the friendly people.

There also were breath-taking, magnificent, and awe-inspiring sunrises and sunsets. I truly loved exploring the beautiful English countryside. I particularly enjoyed the quintessential British hamlets—traditional small settlements with a church, school, post office, and a pub.

One of my favourites was Stratford-upon-Avon, the medieval market town where William Shakespeare was born. Even in the small village schools in Ukraine, we studied translations of Shakespeare. So, I was thrilled to visit the home of one of the greatest writers in the English language, the world's most distinguished dramatist and England's national poet!

Now a museum, Shakespeare's birthplace is a restored 16th-century half-timber house on Hanley Street. It's a simple dwelling, with just the essentials for living, such as beds, chairs, a fireplace, and a chest of drawers. Shakespeare's father John was a middle-class glove maker and wool dealer, and the family's house was divided into two parts to accommodate John's workshop.

Millions of people come from all over the world to stand in the spot where this great mind sprang forth. The plethora of languages you hear during a visit is a living testimony to Shakespeare's ongoing international appeal. Shakespeare imprinted his name in the world of literature, poetry, and drama. His legacy is eternal—his words of wisdom are beloved. His mark on earth was significant and profound.

Walking down the original stone floors in this 400-year-old house, educating myself about life in 16th-century England, and imagining the medieval British spirit made me think about the footprints we all have the opportunity to leave behind for others. People like Shakespeare inspire us to think bigger about our place on this earth and what we can do.

Whether it's Shakespeare, or anyone else, we need role models to look up to in life—to follow their example in terms of greatness. You don't have to be as famous as Shakespeare for your life to carry great meaning. Having an impact on the world doesn't mean being the best or being famous. It is what you do daily, how you show up in life, and being on your best game that adds meaning to your life and builds your legacy.

Sometimes, it takes as little as a smile or an authentic compliment to sprinkle magic on someone's else's day…

Create The Life You Dream About

What legacy are you going to leave in this world?

> Ask yourself these questions:
> How are you living your life?
> Are you intentionally writing a story with meaning, one that focuses on adding value to humankind?
> These questions require self-reflection. They should be taken seriously, considered thoughtfully, and then reconsidered regularly to make sure you are on track in life. Live a life that matters, be proactive rather than reactive, travel far and wide to learn from others, and take every step in life with intention.
> What would you like people to say about your life at your wake?

"Begin with the end in mind." – **Stephen Covey**

Contemplating your legacy—how you want to be remembered—will help you identify or bring clarity to your dream. Start and engage in the story that matters to you. Your story and your life matter. Remember, your meaning of life will be something you have passion for. Having passion for your dream will give you the wings to fly with it.

Do you have an otaku?

When looking for your meaning of life, it's helpful to also consider your *otaku*. In Seth Gogin's book *Purple Cow*, he talks about a great Japanese word: *otaku*. It's a term for people with obsessive interests.

I love this word, because it's the place where my passion and my gifts come together, so I am relentless in taking action here.

Otaku is my strength zone. It's the place where most of my creativity comes into play. It's the place where I can lose myself for hours and I know I am making a difference, not just doing a good job.

In the modern world we're living in, doing a good job isn't enough. Let's take a small business for example. How many businesses out there produce a good product, deliver a good service, but they struggle to get by and eventually go out of business? Why is this? Because being "good" in a modern world means you're invisible. Good is the enemy of success. Good means average. The market now is overwhelmed with "good" products and services. Any other new good product that appears on the market goes unnoticed. In order to get noticed, you need to be interesting. As Mr. Godin wisely points out, you need to be remarkable! For that, you've got to have an *otaku*.

> **What is your otaku? What excites you about your current work? What makes you do what you do beyond just the money? What makes you unique? What makes you compelling to other people?**

When you have an otaku, you operate from the place of your uniqueness. Having an otaku enables you to stand out from the crowd. It brings attention to you, allowing you to get a natural flow of customers. An otaku differentiates you because you constantly learn and explore and grow. You do what you are truly passionate about. You can't wait to get up in the morning because your otaku is calling you.

With an *otaku*, you're not afraid to go the extra mile; you're not afraid to be bold and courageous. You're not afraid to fail, because you enjoy the process. The journey itself is worth the hassle. Even if you don't get to the desired outcome, you still consider yourself a winner because you gain invaluable experience, you expand your awareness and yourself, and you get a better understanding of what might work next time.

With a little bit of introspection, I believe that everyone can get to the place of their unique *otaku*. It absolutely doesn't mean you need to radically change your life, your job, or your business. But it definitely means that you can improve your life and increase your results. It has been proven by science that we have unlimited potential (Abraham Maslow). Anyone can expand their results to unimaginable heights if they're willing to operate from the place of *otaku*.

Whatever you do, chances are you won't create anything completely new or original, unless you are a scientific inventor, of course. How's that for motivation? But it is true! Whatever industry you're in, you're not alone there. Even Elon Musk wasn't the first inventor of electric cars or space rockets, yet everyone knows his name in these industries. Be inspired by those who came before you and those alongside you.

You don't need to be totally original in what you do, but you absolutely have to be passionate about it. Having an otaku helps you to find a unique approach to presenting or creating great things from the things that already exist.

> **The possibility to become remarkable happens when you bring your uniqueness and your original touch to the product or service you are offering. The way you position yourself and the way you bring your uniqueness and your creativity determines how successful you will be.**

An angel of inspiration

So, when you've found your *otaku* and you know what legacy you want to leave behind, how do you find inspiration to expand and enlarge yourself? For me, it's about making connections with people who are inspiring. Sometimes, random events lead you to make connections that provide the most awe-inspiring revelations.

For me, this happened when a friend recommended I watch a movie called *Gimme Shelter*. It's based on the true and inspiring story of a pregnant teen who escaped her abusive and drug-addicted mother, searched for her biological father, and ended up in a shelter for pregnant women. There, she learned about love and compassion and bonded with like-minded women from similar situations. The shelter became a safe haven she could call home.

The film touched me deeply, and it taught me an important message about life. There is so much suffering in this world, yet there are places that transform and save people's lives through love, compassion, and community support.

When I researched the movie, I discovered the real places and people behind it—Kathy DiFiore and her Several Sources Shelters in Ramsey, NJ. So on a recent trip to New York City, I decided to visit one of the shelters. I wasn't sure what to expect or even whether they'd permit visitors. After all, why would they accept a complete stranger? To my surprise, they were very welcoming, and what I found was a special and unique place of selflessness, compassion, inspiration, and hope against all odds.

It was such a rare gem to find in a world driven by superficial pursuits such as "the selfie" and social media, where some people expose only the glorified highlights of their lives. It might sound judgmental, but this is what I stand for: meaning and substance; not shallowness and pretence. And Kathy is one of the people who has so much meaning.

In the world, there are unforgettable people who you meet once in a lifetime. Those who choose to lead their lives differently. There's something about their energy and presence that inspires others. Kathy DiFiore is one of those people—a selfless woman who has dedicated the past 30 years of her life to helping countless others. Her story, her work, and her mission are a true inspiration for the world.

Kathy dedicates her life to helping those in need by providing shelters for homeless, rejected, and deprived women—giving them hope and dignity. She walks the walk and talks the talk, and she has endured many struggles and challenges in her own life. She was in an abusive marriage herself and was homeless at one point. Kathy has worked with Mother Teresa, changed state housing laws, opened Several Sources Shelters, been honoured by President Ronald Reagan at the White House, and helped to save and rebuild the lives of many women and children.

When I met Kathy, she handed me a copy of her book, *Gimme Love, Gimme Hope, Gimme Shelter*. Curious to know more about her, I began to read and was immediately moved by one of her sayings, "God writes straight in crooked lines". She means that sometimes people are exposed to pain and problems, but there is a reason for it all, and in time, they discover their life purpose because of those difficulties. Like many, Kathy endured many crooked lines in her life, but found her purpose.

When I first entered the house, a little boy kept saying, "Kathy, Kathy," looking at her with love and devotion. I'll never forget that image; in just a few words, his expression taught me about Kathy DiFiore, her mission, and her life. So much love from just one small child. Then I realised that there were hundreds of babies and children who had been there over the years and expressed just as much unconditional love and devotion for her. Their photos were everywhere around the shelter. It was empowering.

In the shelter, I saw a statue of Jesus that Mother Teresa had given to Kathy. The statue had no hands, which sparked my curiosity. I asked why, and Kathy's response was, "We have to become the hands to help people". This powerful concept got me thinking about my own life and what was I doing with my "hands" to help others. Perhaps we can all do more to help others.

On a table, I noticed a book about angels. I picked it up and looked at it for a minute, flipping through the images of holy angels. Later, as I was leaving the shelter, I was thinking, *Kathy DiFiore is definitely one of those holy angels that make this world a better place.*

What difference do you make in your life and how do you influence the lives of others? When you're looking for meaning in your life, look to people who are inspiring, who add value to the world, and who create meaning for others.

I love studying successful people, but Kathy taught me a new definition of success—one focused on saving and enhancing other people's lives, rather than accomplishing things for themselves. Where success turns into significance, where you live not just for yourself but for others as well. Any story of inspiration begins with giving. If you do it with an open, genuine heart, you'll be amazed by the rewards and fulfilment that your life will provide to you.

"*Success is when I add value to myself. Significance is when I add value to others.*" –**John Maxwell**

Summary

Life without a meaning isn't worth living. You have the power to define your life and what meaning it acquires. Look for figures of inspiration in history, art, literature, or people from everyday life. Follow their example to live your best to your highest potential. Learn to live life with fulfilment. Think of your legacy—how you wish to be remembered—and your *otaku*. It will help you gain more clarity on your life purpose, on your dream, and it will enhance the meaning of your life.

CHAPTER 6

The Importance of Self-Development

There is a story about a child in Rome who spent hours watching a strange artist working intently. Finally, the boy spoke, "Signore, *why* are you hitting that rock?" At this point, Michelangelo looked up from his work and answered, "Because there is an angel inside and he wants to come out".

Michelangelo's magnificent sculptures have inspired people throughout the centuries. His skill, the depth of emotion he rendered, and his fine craftsmanship are incredible. It's amazing how simple his secret was though: he just visualised a masterpiece in the rock, and with the help of a hammer and chisel, he removed everything that was covering it up. That's it!

There are beautiful masterpieces everywhere—especially in our heart. We have unlimited potential. We have personal power. But how can we adopt a similar approach to Michelangelo to uncover our angel? It's very simple: to claim these treasures, to fulfil our life purpose, and to achieve our highest potential, we must engage in personal growth and development. So, in this chapter, we'll look at growth and development of the self.

Uncovering your personal angel

On my own personal journey, I've found that it's not always easy to chip away at the façade we create for ourselves and that others place upon us. But with faith and time, we can reveal the core of our true inner potential. For example, I was born in a small Ukrainian village, struggled early on at school, faced financial challenges, and experienced the difficulties of being an immigrant in the USA all by myself. But rather than letting these circumstances define my world, I shaped my own image of who I would become and chiselled away at the ingrained patterns and behaviours that threatened to keep me stuck in the quarry. Persistence and effort eventually paid off for me.

It takes time, effort, and hard work to uncover your own personal angel. Sometimes, along the way, it's hard to see the masterpiece in the rock, but that vision of your inner angel is what enables you to become anything or anyone you desire in life. And no doubt, it takes courage to uncover that personal power within.

Most people don't have the vision; they don't have the dream. They aren't willing to take the hammer and chisel and chip away at the layers blocking their true potential. They refuse to take action and grow. **Don't be one of those people.** Have faith that you are whole and complete underneath all of the unnecessary outer layers of rock, which for us means our limiting beliefs, negativity, and self-doubt. Chip away at those outer layers by embracing personal development and growth. Engage in the process of self-improvement.

My personal growth journey involves reading self-help books, attending mind-expanding conferences and seminars, surrounding myself with people who are more successful than me so I can learn from them and model their success, and working on my limiting belief system (the inner voices telling me what I can't do). It was an exhilarating journey of gaining higher levels of self-awareness, and it still is, as each day I continue to grow and develop myself. Your self-development journey might be similar to mine or different.

However, you've got to bear in mind that while there is a masterpiece inside you, masterpieces are not created overnight. Go easy on yourself when you don't get the desired outcomes straight away, and trust in the value of the process. Growth happens *day by day*, not in a day.

We can inspire ourselves if we simply appreciate ourselves, celebrate the small every-day victories, and keep our eyes on our aspired goals.

> **In your life, you'll use the hammer and the chisel combined with personal development and taking action to achieve your goal or vision. Keep hitting the rock until the 'angel' emerges.**

Why does self-development begin with feeling you are enough?

It might sound counterintuitive, but before you can grow and develop, you need to feel that you are enough as you are. This means not comparing yourself to other people or looking down on yourself. I learned this after a few years of living in the USA, before I discovered my dream of becoming a speaker or gained clarity on designing my life.

What happened was I met the love of my life. Or at least that's what I thought. My "prince charming" was a handsome Russian guy, who was kind, generous, intelligent, funny, and really successful. He introduced me to the luxurious side of life. And he treated me really well initially. It was a huge shift for a girl who was born and raised in a poor village to suddenly taste the life of limos and private jets.

He lived by the principle of choosing only the best in life. And I was happy thinking of myself as a princess from a fairy tale, who would soon step out of her rags and into riches. I will always be grateful to him for raising my life standards, as he inspired me to think bigger. However, the happiness was only fleeting and soon turned into moral torture.

You see, I really loved the guy for who he was—not for what he had. Of course, wealth was a nice addition to an amazing man. However, when we first met, I didn't know what he did or the fact that he was rich. I admired his confidence, his sharp thinking, and his sense of humour. He was so well-grounded, and an enormous power came from within him. At that moment, I realised that success in life is attracted to the person you become. And I wanted to become like him—a winner in life.

However, subconsciously I thought less of myself, always comparing my achievements to his. I was always miserable, because I felt like I had achieved nothing and he had achieved everything. Besides my youth and beauty, in my mind I had nothing else to offer. All of my aspirations for a better life seemed so miserable in contrast to his already sky-scraping success. I felt like I wasn't enough. At the time, I was working in a restaurant, while he was remotely managing his empire in Russia from his computer. The contrast between our worlds was drastic. And it was depressing for me.

That wasn't the only problem in our relationship. After about six months, I realised that he was seeing other women, and I wasn't his significant other—I was just part of him enjoying life. I hoped he would change. And I tried to change myself to become his only one... But eventually, I realised that he never loved me and never would. After 18 months of being on and off, we broke up. I felt like I died. And a piece of me died forever. A part of me that was insecure and dependent on outside validation to prove my own worthiness.

Later, I realised that this drama was a blessing in disguise. But at the time, I was heartbroken and looking for a way to get rid of my personal demons. So I pulled the remaining pieces of my life together and started rebuilding my heart and mind. I got involved in personal development and dived deep into personal growth. I became aware that I had serious self-worth issues. I didn't love myself. I didn't think of myself as being enough. And I was placing my personal value **outside** of me.

So, I read inspirational books that fed my mind and cured my soul, and bought self-help growth programs that inspired me to think bigger and recognise my personal power. Little by little, I learned to love myself and see my personal worthiness as something that is not dependent on outside circumstances or other people's validation.

By losing myself, I gained myself. This unfortunate personal drama actually held a perfect place in my life, as it reminded me of my self-worth the hard way. It helped me to build my self-confidence. I attracted that man for a reason: to teach me that I was enough. As the story of my life goes, that was my inspiration through desperation.

My journey of self-discovery had begun. It took me time to realise that I was the only one who could save myself. What I was searching for all around had always been buried deep within the dust of my soul and the marrow of my bones.

> **In order to be a princess, you don't need to be rescued by a prince. You've got to claim that status for yourself. You have to win yourself before you win the world. Before you believe in your dream, you need to believe in yourself and believe that you can do it.**

"People are like stained-glass windows. They sparkle and shine, but when darkness sets in, their true beauty is revealed only if there is light within." – **Jean Houston**

A tale of triumph

Like many people, I love fairy tales. They carry universal appeal, with profound and deep teachings. The draw is much more than just tales of "good vs. evil" with a happy ending. By opening the curtains on the mysterious and magical, fairy tales help us better understand our own life. They help to bring out the best in us and build our faith in miracles. They reflect our aspirations and dreams, elevate our spirit, inspire our soul, and provide valuable lessons. For example, the Cinderella story reveals deep wisdom and uncovers the secret of how to connect with our inner self and make miracles happen.

Cinderella, a kind sweetheart, is unfortunate to live with her wicked stepmother and stepsisters, who never miss a chance to mock or humiliate her. However, Cinderella's benevolence and genuine heart, hard work and perseverance, and positive attitude and optimism bring much virtue and merit to her personality.

You probably know how the story unfolds: a young girl cleans off the ashes after being forced to sleep on the floor near the fireplace, and with the help of her magical fairy godmother, puts on a beautiful dress, arrives gracefully in a beautiful carriage to a ball taking place at the palace, and meets the prince, who is enamoured with her.

As the clock strikes midnight, Cinderella loses her glass slipper in a rush to get home before the magic spell breaks. The prince uses the slipper to find her, then they get married, and conquer all challenges—including envy, jealousy, and greed—and live happily ever after.

On the surface, it's a graceful female journey from a maid to a princess. However, the story wouldn't be as powerful and inspiring in the world of art, literature, and movies if it focused only on her elegance, beauty, love, genuineness, and kind heart.

The deep fascination with this fairy tale lies in the fact that Cinderella, despite her miserable outside circumstances, never plays the role of a victim. She never complains about her unfair treatment and her wretched destiny, and she never blames her family members (although they were evil) or outside circumstances.

Releasing the victim mentality

How many people do you know who blame everyone and everything for their perceived miserable existence, not realising that by having this attitude, they attract more of what they resist? In contrast, Cinderella was happy and hopeful in her unhappy surroundings. She subconsciously believed in her powerful inner self and became connected to universal grace through her open loving heart and optimistic attitude.

Cinderella had nothing, but she had everything with her positive perspective on life. She became the princess long before she changed her appearance and the prince fell in love with her. She showed up at the ball and she attracted the prince because of *who she was*. In reality, those who wait for someone to rescue or fix them without doing anything themselves will develop the wrong attitude in life and will always remain in that situation.

> **If you rely on someone else to come and save you, then you remain passive and angry, stuck in your current circumstances. We have no control over our external circumstances; we can't change them, but we can change what they mean to us and our attitude toward them. We can be in charge of our inner world, which will shape our outside "reality".**

Miracles happen on the inside; what we see outside is merely a reflection of the inner transformation. Magic operates at the soul level. The appearance of a fairy in a story is a metaphor for the bridge between our dreams and their manifestation from the soul. It is a graceful tap on our shoulder from the creative source of the universe.

Even when the fairy appeared to Cinderella, she didn't create anything new. She just transformed something that already existed. She didn't order the dress out of catalogue; she transformed Cinderella's old rags into a ball gown. She didn't order a limo; she turned a pumpkin into a coach and mice into horsemen. The magic happened, but was it really magic? Or was it the natural grace of the universe? Cinderella had everything she needed within her and around her—just in disguise.

Rags-to-riches stories serve as powerful inspiration that our dreams do come true. However, they acquire shape and gain energy internally. Major transformations always happen at the soul level first. What we observe in the material realm is just the side effects of this inner magic working.

> **We are all princes and princesses, whatever life path we are on. Some have embraced their true royal self, some are still searching, and others are in disguise. The recipe for success is simple: be kind and humble, open your heart, have a positive attitude, take responsibility, don't complain, connect to your inner self with your deepest aspirations, and pursue your happiness and dreams. Miracles will follow.**

Our beliefs drive our behaviour

On my self-development path, I started investing in personal growth programs. It helped me rebuild my self-worth. Often, I was spending way beyond my means or what my pay rate would allow.

However, if you're willing to bet on yourself, then you automatically increase your personal value, because you tell yourself you must be worthy to be spending this money on yourself. It's not an overnight transformation, but if you're committed to the magic of process, then you will enjoy the rewards.

I started surrounding myself with high achievers—learning, growing, and expanding myself, building my vision. I was mesmerised by the beautiful principles, insights, and empowering beliefs those guru masters shared about life, freedom, achievement, success, significance, and happiness. But at the same time, I was frustrated. *Why was that?*

Because I couldn't figure out why those principles worked for everyone else but me. Have you ever felt like that? I was working with a coach at the time, and one day I said to her, "Angelique, I'm putting so much effort into changing my life, but nothing changes. My life is so hard! Why is that?" She replied, "Maybe, you should stop saying that your life is hard. That is deeply engraved in your subconscious mind and it shapes your reality. Have you ever thought about that?"

I did think about it. It turned out she was right. I loved the empowering beliefs I read or heard about, but they were in conflict with the disempowering negative beliefs that were subconsciously running my life. All of our results stem from our beliefs.

Looking back at myself in Ukraine, I was someone who wanted more, who didn't settle for a poor and unconscious life. I came from humble beginnings and a place where there was a victim psychology that life was hard, but you just have to deal with it. Words such as *success, achievement, greatness,* and *dreams* were not part of our consciousness, let alone our vocabulary.

Even though I had broken through that reality and come to the USA, I had brought with me deep-seated negative beliefs that I wasn't even aware of, and they were still running my life. These beliefs were things like *life is tough, you must have a special blessing and unique talents in order to have a great life, you've got to be lucky, you've got to work really hard.* Those limitations subconsciously sabotaged my life. On the outside, I wanted to create a better life, but on the inside, I didn't believe I could, and I didn't believe that I was enough.

A key aspect of personal growth is working on your belief system, which elevates your thinking, creates determination, transforms you and your character, and then everything else falls into place. Because our beliefs drive our behaviour. Changing our beliefs, how we perceive life, and how we see ourselves builds our character, resourcefulness, and determines the actions we take.

Because of my limitations in my mind and my lack of self-belief, I was sabotaging my achievements. When I discovered my dream of becoming an inspirational speaker, I wanted to help people but deep inside, I didn't believe I could. Deep inside, I needed to help myself.

I would tell myself, "Before you try to reach out to others, you have to fix your life first. Do you know how many people are doing what you are trying to do? Do you know that English isn't your first language? You don't have any talents. Are you going to make a fool of yourself?" Let me tell you, **you can't give what you don't have.** That's why I wasn't getting anywhere in my life, because I let those inner limitations direct my actions and behaviour.

The negative chatter that comes from your belief system is the most dangerous, because it destroys your dreams if you don't do anything about it. That ongoing inner battle was deterring me from advancing in life. I took one step forward and then a few steps back.

I loved the ideas and principles I was hearing about life's greatness, but I failed to apply them, because deep inside, I didn't believe in myself and my capabilities. I was entertaining negative thinking. I was continuously failing to go within; therefore, I was going without. I wasn't getting emotionally and spiritually involved with the ideas I was reading about or hearing during seminars. Life gives you what flows through you.

Summary

To get your desired outcomes in life, you need to constantly grow and develop yourself in order to have those qualities that help you succeed in life. To grow, it's fundamental that you first believe in yourself and your capabilities, in your unconditional worthiness as a person. You are enough and you are complete as you are—you just need to chip away at the layers of negative beliefs and limitations you have about yourself to uncover your inner angel, which is already there.

You also don't need anyone to come and rescue you to turn you into a princess. Recognise that the princess is within you—it is in your attitude to life. Release your victim mentality and stop blaming outside circumstances for your life.

CHAPTER 7

The Operations of Your Mind

In this chapter, we'll take a closer look at how our life is created and the important concept that your inner world creates your outer world, an expression you might have heard of before. We'll explore the powerful instrument that controls not just our body, but our entire life. This instrument is our mind. I will show you how to become the conscious creator of your life using your conscious and subconscious mind.

Take a look inside

Imagine your car isn't performing properly—what do you do? Change the paint, polish the tires, and install leather seats? It's not rocket science to understand that cosmetically touching up the car's exterior won't improve its performance. You have to open the bonnet and work on the interior of the car to boost its performance.

Let's open the bonnet of ourselves, where the unseen yet most powerful part resides—the mind. We have been raised to operate and perceive the world through our physical senses. We ignore anything that we can't see, touch, smell, or hear. We rarely give our attention and energy to where our highest power lies. By discarding the unseen, we detract from our ability to recognise, embrace, and live into our potential. Our physical senses provide a very limited and linear perception of the world—the physical, visible side. Yet all of the "magic" happens in the unseen part of ourselves.

> **Our body is the instrument of our mind. Our mind is the movement. And the body is the manifestation of that movement. Our mind is the epicentre of our performance.**

There are two primary parts of the mind: the conscious and the subconscious. The conscious mind is our **thinking mind**, where our ability to reason, our cognitive intelligence or IQ, and our current level of awareness lie. This part has the capacity to accept or reject any idea received from the outside through our physical senses. All the thoughts entertained in our conscious mind are created by our imagination.

The subconscious mind is our **emotional mind**. This part helps us to feel life and react to life. It's a massive memory bank, where all of our beliefs, habits, and values are stored. While the conscious mind is the source of our intelligence, cognitive abilities, or IQ, our subconscious mind is the source of our emotional (EQ) and spiritual intelligence (SQ). Our EQ and SQ have a much bigger influence in our success and happiness than our IQ.

The interesting thing about our subconscious mind is that it operates in every cell of our body, simultaneously performing millions of functions to ensure the correct operation of our body. Millions of neurons with different roles are running our body without our conscious involvement. This is only scratching the surface of its capacity. When we stop to think and look around us and we are really aware, then we begin to understand the magnitude and power that is at play within us.

The subconscious mind knows **no limits other than those we impose on it**. Unlike our conscious mind, our subconscious mind has no ability to reject or deny ideas. It is entirely deductive in nature. The subconscious mind only accepts ideas impressed by our reasoning mind. It has no capacity to identify what serves us and what is appropriate in any particular situation. It has no situational awareness.

There is a great story I want to share with you about self-limitations…

A man was passing by some elephants. He suddenly stopped, puzzled by what he saw. These huge creatures were being held by just a small rope tied to their front legs. There were no chains or cages. It was evident that the elephants could break away from the ropes they were tied to at any time, but for some reason, they didn't. The man saw a trainer nearby and asked him why the beautiful, magnificent animals just stood there, and made no attempt to break free.

"Well," the trainer replied, "when they are very young and much smaller, we used the same size rope to tie them and at that age, it was enough to hold them. As they grow up, they are conditioned to believe they cannot break away. They believe the rope can still hold them, so they never try to break free." The man was astonished. These animals could break free from their bonds at any time, but because they believed they couldn't, they were stuck right where they were.

Like the elephants, how many of us go through life hanging on to the negative voice that we cannot do something simply because we failed at it once before? **–Author unknown**

Why does this programming get created?

Understanding the mechanics of your mind should help you understand how your conditions and circumstances play out in your life. Any thought or idea that we consciously focus on over and over again becomes fixed and forms our learned behaviour, which are commonly called habits. A group of habits are called paradigms, programming, or conditioning.

These are learned behaviours that continue to be expressed without our conscious assistance. They are reactions. We only experience their legacy by means of our results. Learned behaviour is sometimes useful, because we don't have to spend time figuring out how to open the door each time we face one, or tie our shoe laces. At one point in our lives, we had to work it out.

Our subconscious mind is programmed to elicit an automatic action or reaction through repetition. Think of how you learned the alphabet, words, and their meaning, then eventually acquired reading skills. You had to memorise and repeat letters and words. At one point, you had to consciously think what the symbols on paper meant. Now, reading is an automatic behaviour. This is just a simple example of how the subconscious mind gets programmed via conscious involvement and then serves us automatically. Our subconscious mind is programmed to reproduce the learned behaviour when required.

An interesting fact about the difference between the thinking and emotional mind was discovered by neuroscientist Bruce Lipton. According to him, the conscious mind processes 2000 bits per second and the subconscious mind processes 4 billion bits per second. So you can see where most of our power lies. Most of our behaviour happens outside of our conscious awareness, somewhere between 75% – 90%.

Every thought that is accepted by your conscious mind is automatically accepted by your subconscious mind. Those thoughts cause feelings or vibrations, and the feelings and vibrations are expressed through a physical medium that the subconscious controls—the body. The body is moved based on particular emotions. Emotion is the energy in motion. Consequently, your body is moved into taking an action, which then create the results in your personal and professional life. This is the natural law of cause and effect. That's how your thinking creates your reality.

The interplay of thoughts, feelings, and actions in human psychology is what creates your attitude to life. Your attitude is the primary cause of the results you get. That's why it's so important to have a positive attitude.

> **Your attitude (your thoughts, feelings, and actions) are responsible for every single result you get in your life. What attitude do you have towards your life?**

We falsely believe that our existing results represent our potential. That is the most crippling interpretation that a person can make about their life. Here is the truth: **our existing results do not represent our potential.** They represent our current awareness of our potential. As you continue to grow and develop yourself, you will understand what Abraham Maslow meant when he said that *our potential is infinite.*

Our existing results represent the quality of our thinking up until this point in our life. There are three levels of creation: thoughts, feelings, and actions. So, in order to improve your results, you have to improve the quality of your thinking. Improving the quality of your thinking and improving your performance happens through *awareness*.

> **Your task is to increase your awareness. Bring a conscious understanding to what kind of thoughts you choose to entertain on a daily basis, because these form your conditioning or your subconscious mind, which automatically makes you behave and respond to life in a certain way.**

Our problem is that all of our current attention and energy is fixated on our current level of performance, and our thoughts are influenced by our results. This becomes an eternal circle: our thoughts are shaped by our existing results, which create the same feelings and vibrations, which move us to make the same actions, creating the same or similar results.

As widely documented, that is the definition of insanity—doing the same thing over and over again and expecting a different result. This is the perfect recipe for mediocrity and desperation in life.

> **To break the cycle, you need to change your programming: your thought and behaviour patterns. Start imprinting your subconscious mind with the thoughts and ideas you wish to experience in your own life. Consciously condition your mind, because your mind is the starting point of transformation in your life.**

There are so many people who know they need to do something about their life, but they keep sabotaging themselves, because deep inside, they don't believe they can do it.

Unless you open the bonnet and fix the mechanics, your car's performance will not improve. And just like the car, you have to open your mind and work on the inner mechanics to improve your performance and your results.

Just like your car runs more smoothly when the mechanics, engine, and wheels are in alignment, your performance in life is better when your thoughts, feelings, and actions are in harmony, so you consciously create your desired outcomes.

> **If you struggle to change or align your thoughts, feelings, and actions, you can hire a life coach. They will help you recognise your limitations and change the operations of your mind. Sometimes it's helpful to have the guidance of a mentor who will help you understand that you are worthy.**

Summary

If you want to fix your outside circumstances, then you need to understand how your mind works and look inside to "fix" your beliefs, as these drive your behaviour and create the results you get. You need to increase your awareness and elevate your consciousness. Your mind is in a constant state of creation. However, for the majority of people, this process is unconscious—that's why they keep getting the same results. Nothing outside you will change until something inside changes.

CHAPTER 8

Winner's Qualities

In order to be successful and create your dream life, you have to develop winner's qualities within your character. In this chapter, we'll look at some winner's qualities, such as being movement-orientated not moment-orientated, being determined, being smart with your time, having courage, celebrating your victories, being authentic, being simple, and being a kind of person who lives, loves, and laughs.

Movement not moment

We live in a fast-paced society. A German proverb says, "The American hour for runs 40 minutes". The majority of people have instant reward expectations. I call these "moment people". They want results now, right here. They want gratification right away to boost their ego. They refuse to accept the universal law of gender (also known as the law of gestation), which says all things need a gestation period. All seeds must germinate before sprouting. All ideas need time to sprout and grow. Our hopes, dreams, and goals all need time to gestate. Nothing happens instantly. This is the inevitable law of creation, that time is required for incubation and manifestation.

With "moment" people, they are never responsible for their life's misfortunes; they find excuses; they are inconsistent; they are driven by outside events; and they think that life should be easy. Therefore, they are stuck and unhappy in their life.

I encourage you to be a **movement** person instead: be responsible, give no excuses, be driven by inside forces, and understand that nothing is easy in life. Life is simple, but it's not easy. There is a difference between looking easy and being easy. Movement people don't ask how long it will take. Because it's going to take longer than you think, and it's going to cost more than you think. Movement people ask how far they can go. Do you understand the difference? Movement people don't hold on to the vision they can handle; they hold on to the vision they are destined for.

Be determined

Don't kill your dream with impatience. I am guilty of that. When I was first taking the baby steps on my entrepreneurial journey, I wanted to see the results right away. That immature stage of hunger was interfering with my winner's spirit. I was frustrated when I couldn't make the sales; when I couldn't get paying clients for my speaking and coaching services. The frustration was blinding my vision and was slowing me down.

Building something from scratch is a tough job. And it requires your investment: your time, energy, money, and soul, and it's usually unrewarded in the beginning. This means you've got to be determined, stick to the process, and do whatever it takes to become the person you wish to become, to create the life you dream about.

Determination is your inside drive; it is the belief in your dream (which is bigger than your current circumstances). Your determination helps you keep your eyes on your vision when things get tough. The result of your determination is persistence. Persistence is about you taking action until you succeed. If determination is your inner force, persistence is your outside force.

People often get excited about something. They get inspired and become motivated. They vigorously take action; they work hard. They seem to have positive thoughts and high expectations about their goal. But then something happens: a roadblock, a problem, some difficulty, and their inner voice starts talking them out of their dream. "Who do you think you are? Do you think you're the only one who's doing this thing? Do you know how many people like you have failed? They were passionate in the beginning, but look what happened in the end…"

This voice goes on and on, becoming stronger and stronger until it becomes unbearable and eventually people give up on their dream. Moment people can't wait; they are impatient; and they aren't strong inside. As a result, they succumb to their personal limitations and fears, and the negative mindset takes over their actions. Although they dream of success, their mindset is set up for failure. Determination and persistence make the difference.

When you encounter a problem, the answer or solution you're looking for might not be on the surface. This is a sign that your dream is worthy and valuable. John Maxwell said, "Everything worthwhile is uphill." Develop determination and persistence. It helps you to develop the attitude of "I can".

> **You don't make things happen through contemplating how you can't make things happen. There is always a reasonable explanation why you can't do something. There is always a reasonable explanation why you can too. It's your choice. When you stick to your goal and your dream, you develop "possibility thinking". Make up your mind to do everything possible to meet your standard of living. Live into your dream before it becomes a reality.**

Persistence and determination within our area of gifts and talents will pave the way to our dreams. Where we focus our attention, that's where we direct our energy and efforts. Focus your attention and energy on the things that matter and don't retreat until you've become the person you have envisioned. Doing so is tough, but extremely rewarding. You have to develop determination about your dream. Keep going and moving toward your dream, and when you reach it, then dream bigger.

Be smart with your time

When I was at one of the leadership conferences, I was touched by one of the speakers who was talking about how we use our time. That speaker said, "Some people accomplish more in a week than others in a year." I needed to hear that message because it reminded me of how ineffective I was with my time. We might be different in our talents, our resources, our beliefs, or our programming. But the only resource we have in an equal amount is time.

Bill Gates has the same 24 hours in a day as you and I! However, what we do with it determines everything. Mostly, people waste their time on unnecessary things. I was guilty of that too. I still am sometimes. A lot of times, I caught myself thinking that I'm not doing the things I need to be doing. Has this ever happened to you?

> **To use your time wisely, consider these questions:**
> **What do you do on a daily basis?**
> **What's your habitual routine?**
> **Does it serve you?**
> **Do you keep track of your progress?**
> **Do you write things down that need to be done?**
> **Where does your attention go?**

When I started asking myself these questions, I started shifting my mind and my daily activities. Doing this is all personal growth. Small incremental changes within your subconsciousness play a defining role in your performance. As you've seen, our inner world or our subconscious (thoughts, beliefs, convictions, habits) creates our outer world.

> **I'm not saying you should stop watching TV or delete your Facebook, but I highly encourage you to be consciously aware of where and how you spend your time. When you feel like you're wasting your time (my gut always tells me so), think about what you could be doing right now that will bring you closer to your dreams.**

I'm still fighting the bad habit of spending too much time on social media though. Puppies are cute, cats are silly, and babies are adorable, but in the end, it literally kills our time, you know. When you stop and think about the benefit of social media or TV, you realise there isn't much. But as humans, we like being entertained.

A powerful woman I know called Jennifer discovered her true life calling and passion to help people. She was working full time at corporate job at the time. So, she would wake up every morning at 4 am and spend two to three hours working on her dream business before going to work. Talking about an effective usage of time! That was inspiring to me.

I am not encouraging you to be sleep-deprived of course, but maybe cutting down how often you watch TV will help you find time to work on your dream?

> **There is no such thing as time management. There is management of you. You decide how you are going to use your 24 hours and what you want to achieve every day. To use our time effectively, you need to establish healthy and effective discipline.**
> - What do you do when you wake up?
> - What are your priorities during the day?
> - How do you keep track of the progress you've achieved?

Now, my primary focus for my daily activities is directed toward speaking (preparing my speeches, practicing them, watching and learning from world-class speakers), writing (stimulating my thinking and my creativity), and building my business.

There's an insightful dialogue between a master of martial arts and one of his students:

The Student (S), "Why I am not advancing in my technique master?"

The Teacher (T), "Have you seen the sunset when the seagulls fly flaming across the plain?"

S, "Yes, master!"

T, "And the water from the waterfall hitting the rock without achieving anything?"

S, "Yes, master!"

T, "And the moon reflecting on calm water?"

S, "Yes, master!"

T, "There is your problem. You keep watching stupid stuff instead of practicing!"

It is much easier to say yes than to say no. Say no to things that don't serve you. When you learn to say no to the things that are not on your priority list, you become a leader of your life. You have to think on the front end about where and how you're using your time. Think of it this way, you can't get your time back. So use it wisely.

Have courage

"Courage is going from failure to failure without losing enthusiasm." – **Winston Churchill**

Having inspiration is fun, isn't it? It's that initial moment of creation when you give yourself permission to have a dream or a goal. That spark is usually accompanied by feelings of determination, optimism, passion, and motivation. Along your journey to your dreams, it's important to have is courage. According to Elizabeth Gilbert, courage is what separates a mundane existence from a more enchanted one.

Courage comes from Latin word *Cor*, which means heart. So, having courage is bringing forth the power from your heart that makes all things possible and challenges enjoyable.

To be courageous, you need to have your heart set on whatever you aspire to make happen—on your dream. Having that courage from your heart will help you to stay on track, and overcome all the difficulties. Because difficulties **will** happen. If it wasn't difficult to create things, everyone would do it, and it wouldn't be special or interesting.

We all fail. In my very first speaking experience, I failed. When I was 9 years old, I was asked to recite a poem at church. I don't remember what the poem was about, but I remember the meticulous work: learning it and practicing it. On Sunday morning, I was prepared: I knew the rhyme by heart, and I had a backup plan: I had a piece of paper with a poem written on it tucked in the sleeve of my sweater, just in case.

But when I got on "stage", I realised that everybody was looking at me. I couldn't predict that, as I'd never done it before. The audience seemed huge to me. But in fact, there were about 30, maybe 40 people at most. At that moment, I realised what the fear of public speaking was. My knees were shaking, and I had a million thoughts in my mind, none of which I remember. I'd never had such an experience before.

If I'd known what I would have to go through, I wouldn't have taken the role. But it was too late to retreat. So I started speaking, and then after a few lines, I realised that I couldn't remember what came next. *Oh, lord help me!* I thought. Out of all places I was in church. Apparently, God was busy on a more important occasion. I held on to that piece of paper, but I couldn't move to take it out, because my mind and my body were frozen. And everybody kept looking at me…

Have you ever experienced that—when a short period of time seems like forever? Those few seconds were eternity for me. Then I just ran away. I failed miserably. However, it didn't stop me from becoming a professional speaker later in my life.

> **Don't let setbacks break your spirit. Your mistakes and failures should not define who you are. Many people give up on their dreams because they lack the strength of their character, which is built up by courage to keep going despite failures.**

When I became part of the John Maxwell team, I had a very clear intention to become a professional motivational speaker. I had been a member of toastmasters for a year and had been manically practicing my speeches and mastering my speaking craft. But nothing had satisfied my hunger yet.

In August 2015, I attended the International Maxwell certification training. I loved the event, and everything about it: the people, the energy, and the atmosphere. But most of all, I was mesmerised by the powerful speakers. They were so confident and full of grace when sharing their transformational message. I could clearly see the transformation happening in front of my own eyes. It was magical.

Personal growth live events are my healthy drug. It's amazing how inspired and insightful people get during those live events. They help you realign with your life purpose and see that all of your challenges have a perfect place on your journey, because if it wasn't for these experiences, you wouldn't be where you are now. As Steve Jobs said, "You cannot connect the dots looking forward. You can only connect them looking backwards. But the dots will always connect for you."

In that life training, I knew for sure that my dots were connecting right that moment. I could see myself clearly on that beautiful stage, with a microphone, with a happy and smiley face in front of thousands of people, confident, and in my sweet spot. I vividly pictured my dream coming true. But at the same time, I started hearing the negative voices in my head saying "How am I going to get on that stage? I don't have any talent or gifts. I don't have much speaking experience. I don't have transformational messages. English isn't my first language, for goodness sake. Who am I to be selected to speak at the International Maxwell certification training?"

> **But that negative chatter, those limitations, only exist in your head and they mean nothing if your dream comes from your heart—if it is a representation of your identity. There will always be doubts, but you've got to have courage.**

Six months later, after hard work, determination, and persistence, I was one of only five people selected to be on that stage. I had the honour and the privilege not only to share my message with about 2000 people from more than 50 different countries in the world, which was magical, but also to share the stage with John Maxwell, Nick Veicjic, and other world-class powerful speakers.

Courage pushes us to take advantage of opportunities that we perhaps didn't even see before, or that we discounted as being too risky. Going after our dreams compels us to pick ourselves up after things go wrong and try a different approach. There is never a straight line to your dreams. Have courage to go all the way to your dreams. Because we were created out of greatness to live a life of greatness.

I have made many mistakes, experienced failures, and done things that I'm not proud of. However, I am a human being: no better or worse than each and every one of you. I didn't allow my many failures to break me—I channelled them to push me forward. I've always had my dreams ahead of me as a guide and a direction on my life's journey. I have a courage, growth-oriented mentality, a hopeful spirit, and always take action.

Celebrate your victories

"The more you celebrate your life, the more there is to celebrate in your life." – **Oprah Winfrey**

Despite my achievements, I am not where I wish to be in my business. I have always put high demands on myself and had high standards for my life. But as the saying goes, "Always be grateful, but never be satisfied." When I look back, I can see that I've grown so much and I've achieved a lot, which I am very grateful for.

Visiting my hometown in Ukraine helped me to recognise and appreciate the distance I've conquered on my life's journey and give myself credit. When I went there, I felt like I didn't fit into that community anymore. The local residents told me that I am extremely lucky. I've never thought of myself this way, however it made me realise that I have grown so much. It's easy to accept praise from someone else when they tell you how great you are, easier than recognising your value yourself, but you have to give yourself credit. Of course, be humble in life, but self-encouragement is essential for success too.

> **How often do you give yourself credit? Celebrate your victories: big and small. Celebrate the small wins and progress versus perfection. Celebrate even the tiniest victories. By allowing yourself to celebrate your wins, however small, your brain craves more of that and you drive yourself to achieve what you desire. If you want to stay fired up, develop a truly focused mindset, feel emotionally alive, feel inspired, develop higher levels of drive, and stay on your best game.**

Our brains are hard-wired for negativity, for ingratitude. Historically, our brains have developed a negativity bias. We are always on the lookout for danger in our environment. That is what helped us to survive thousands of years ago. Even now, subconsciously we train our brain to focus on what went wrong versus our progress and what went right. But that doesn't mean you have to give in to it—you can change your mindset to one of positivity.

Be you, not a title

To be a winner, you just have to be *you*. The world needs you. Now you have to **do your best**, to the best of your ability, using all that you've got. You don't need to be *the best*, the number one compared to anyone else—you have **to be the best compared to you**.

This means you don't need a title to be brilliant. I have always been amazed by the successful stories of people who dropped out of school and achieved enormous heights. They strengthened my faith, as I dropped out of college myself. It was a very tough decision that I kicked myself for years after. The choice was whether to go back to Ukraine and continue my education or to stay in the USA and pursue my dreams. As you know, I stayed in the land of opportunity. But the limitation "I don't have a degree" pulled me backward. Even though it only existed in my mind, it created visible obstacles.

I got this limitation out of my system by learning from those who have made incredible achievements in life without an academic background. Eventually, I realised that a degree has nothing to do with your success. There are many intelligent but broke people. There are many rich people without academic degrees.

Sure, education and knowledge are crucial parts of life mastery, but traditional schools don't teach you the importance of applying the knowledge. They don't teach you *how* to think; they teach you *what* to think. School gives you a lot of valuable information, which you forget after a couple of years.

So at one point, I stopped asking myself whether I was qualified to do something, and I just *did it*. Even now, as I am writing this book, I catch myself with thoughts that I might not be qualified and experienced enough. But that doesn't matter anymore. Because I've got something to say. I want to inspire people to pursue their dreams and to believe in themselves. And that makes a difference.

No matter what you do, all people want is you and your truth. A genuine, authentic expression of you. Be, expand, and express your light.

Jim Carrey once made a profound statement. He said, "*I was going to go into the world and do something that is bigger than myself, until someone smarter than me made me understand that there is nothing bigger than myself.*"

Be simple

Through my speaking experience, I learned the lesson of simplicity. Do you like simplicity? Most people love it when everything is simple. It's easier to live your life that way. The world is complex, but making your life simple creates a more comfortable living. This principle applies to all spheres in life. But as a speaker, I am going to focus on the power of simplicity in communication.

As John Maxwell says, in communication, the cookies need to be on the lower shelf. When you put them too high, it's difficult for people to reach them, and they get disengaged. We love listening to something that's not only educational and useful for us, but also interesting and easy to grasp.

Why do you think the *Books for Dummies* series had such enormous success? Does it mean that only dumb people read them? Not at all! Besides the funny name, the books have a deeper meaning. Life is so complicated already that when someone delivers something easy and simple, people are attracted to it.

Remember your boring school or college professors? Most likely, they were very smart, academically smart, but their delivery and their presentations were dry and lifeless. There is a tendency for educators to take simple things and make them complicated. On the other hand, communicators take complicated things and make them simple.

Explaining complicated phenomena in simple and easy to grasp terms is true mastery. My school teachers in physics, mathematics, and natural science were always so complicated to understand. Some of their explanations were a cure for insomnia. That's why I never liked or learned those subjects. Easy delivery is the secret of connection!

In my public speaking experience, I've noticed that the simpler I present any teaching point, the more engaged the audience is. When I share a personal story to illustrate the point I want to make, I show people what I did instead of telling them about the latest psychological research. That way, people go on emotional journey to grasp a certain idea. And it works really well.

I connect with the audience when I share something that pertains to the simple things in life, such as love, happiness, hope, significance, and dreams. And that inspires people. I believe that you can't be inspirational if you make your presentation complicated and overwhelming with sophisticated and complex vocabulary. People are attracted to simple things that can help them in their life.

People buy into something that is real, authentic, and imperfect faster than they buy into something impeccable, perfect, and flawless. When I first started motivational speaking, I thought I had to focus only on my success, trying to impress people. I have had many achievements, but I am a human being like everyone else, so I have also made tons of mistakes and many failures. So why try to impress people? They are concerned with themselves, with their own life. Then, I learned to be who I am, and I accepted myself and my mistakes as they played a defining role in my resourcefulness. And now I share it with the world.

Our existence in this world comes down to this statement: human beings look for pleasure and try to avoid pain. Human behaviour and actions are controlled by these two basic needs. When I create a pleasant experience while people listen to my speech, I create a win-win situation. People are learning, and they are having an enjoyable experience. And that is the biggest payoff for a speaker.

Whether you are speaking in public or not, this suggestion is helpful in your life. What is my recipe?

> **Be simple, have a smile, be genuine. Put the cookies on the lower shelf. People love cookies. They love it even more when they can easily reach them.**

Live. Love. Laugh.

I am so grateful for my life and all the blessings I have in it. But my biggest blessing is my best friend, my biggest encourager, my soul mate, my lover, and my husband. I call him my English Price Charming for obvious reasons. He is British and he is charming. He is the reason why I moved to rainy England from sunny Miami.

We live in the beautiful English countryside, frequently travel around the world, love what we do, and love each other dearly. Very often, I get "pinch me" moments because I am getting to enjoy my dream life. When I say "You can make your dreams a reality", I mean it.

My husband has all the qualities of my ideal man: sharp thinking, intellect, determination, persistence, appreciation for life, positive attitude, generosity, kindness, and a big, loving heart. Like every human being, he has some shortcomings, but his virtues far outweigh his flaws. Christian is extremely successful, well-grounded, and ridiculously handsome.

He also has an amazing sense of humour, and he makes me laugh all the time and giggle like a child. We have a sign in our kitchen that says "A day without laughter is a day wasted". Let me tell you, we don't waste our days. Laugher is a gift to humanity!

My husband usually says, "I've conquered my ego after I've humbly accepted I am the most sexually attractive man on earth"

As a loving wife I try to entertain his middle age delusion:)

Even the day we got married, he made me laugh. After exchanging our vows, the notary said, "Now it's time to exchange rings." Christian pulled out a blue box with a Haribo ring in it! I started laughing.

The notary didn't realise it was a candy ring and continued in a serious tone, "Repeat after me. I will wear this ring as a sign of my love and the giving of that love will last us the rest of our lives." I couldn't contain myself at that point and said, "I highly doubt it will last us for the rest of our lives, as I might eat it!" Christian looked at me with a smile and said, "Oh, you want a real ring? I am sorry!"

So, he pulled out the second box and took out a plastic ring. I didn't stop laughing. The third box came out and nobody knew what to expect…but the third attempt was perfect. It was a beautiful moment. I was the happiest girl on earth at that moment, and I still am.

> **The sparkles don't end after the wedding day though. Remember to sprinkle magic on each other every day with care, love, and jokes. It doesn't take much to create happiness.**

Ladies, real men do exist. It perplexes me when single women say, "Great men are either married, taken, or don't exist." Nothing could be further from the truth. But your beliefs create your reality. If that's what you think, that all the great men are taken, then that's what you are going to attract: taken or married men that are not available to you.

If you're looking for your Prince Charming, you just need to create your own fairy tale. You just have to know **who** you want to attract in your life. You need to visualise your perfect love story, and it has to make you feel good. Don't limit yourself by aiming for the perfect man though. Real men aren't perfect, but they do have many more virtues than flaws. My husband treats me like a queen. Because that's what a king does. Don't settle for someone who treats you badly.

Don't be impatient—it will happen when you are ready and happy with yourself. It is the power of love mixed with the law of attraction that creates magic. My husband and I were not "looking" for each other, per say. We attracted each other. Just like in the Cinderella story, nobody is going to rescue you.

Your Prince Charming is out there, but don't limit yourself by thinking he must be around the corner. When I met Christian, I was a Ukrainian girl who met a British guy in the USA and then I moved to England with him. While we were dating, for a year and a half we travelled back and forth from Florida to England. **Love has no boundaries.**

Don't forget that love comes in different shapes and forms too. I was extremely happy to connect with Christian's two children from his previous marriage. They spend weekends with us, and that connection grew into love. They are amazing, and we have plenty of fun together. I believe we need to keep that inner child within us, no matter how old we are. We need to have fun, be silly, and be joyful.

Each day, I wake up grateful for the amazing life I get to enjoy, being an author, a speaker, and a happy wife. I'm so glad I've always had the highest standards in my life, which allowed me not to settle for less, but to attract my Prince Charming and to live my dream life.

Life is full of wonder. Live. Love. Laugh.

Summary

You can develop these winning qualities in your personality to enjoy your life and be a successful person. Be determined—ask yourself not "how long it is going to take?", but "how far I can go?" Be smart with your time and your priorities, be authentic, and always live, love, and laugh.

Last Words

Now it's time for you to start creating your dream life. When you start this journey, know that it's okay to be scared. It's okay not to have any clarity. It's okay if you don't know how to create it. But you have to stay true to yourself and your dream. Believe me, if you're determined and you hold on to your dream and you keep moving toward it, then it will be yours.

By the way, as I am writing this, I am an American Citizen! Giving the pledge of allegiance to the flag of the United States of America was one of the most fascinating moments in my life mixed with an intoxicating sense of pride, gratitude, and achievement! Very humbling, blessed and joyful moment that was that will stay with me forever!

What is your dream?

You can't change your past, but you can always shape your future by acting today. You have to act now. If you wait for a better time or better circumstances, you will never do it. Life is in session now. Are you present?

Everyone wants to be successful. I haven't met anybody who doesn't want to be successful. There is something magical and captivating behind the word "success". However, hardly anyone is ready to do what it takes to achieve it. You have to work on achieving success. Success goes way beyond and above money.

Create The Life You Dream About

Although money is important—it doesn't define who you are or what you can achieve in life. Over the years of studying successful people, I realised that success leaves clues. It all starts and ends with you and your mind. If you want to change your life, you have to change your mind.

The difference between achievers and underachievers is in the size of their aspirations and dreams. You've got to fill your mind with success files. Everything is an idea at the beginning. So, if your idea is small or negative, its manifestation will not get bigger or become positive. Thinking big means thinking from a place of possibility, not limitations. Don't confuse thinking big with taking big actions. You can think big yet take small steps and tiny actions to get there.

To get your dream life, you need to release your victim mentality, and stop blaming the outside world for your misfortunes. If you do this, you deprive yourself of your power to change your circumstances. So take responsibility over everything that happens to you: both good and bad. By accepting what is, you can create what could be.

People pray for the right circumstances and the right time to come, believing that this is the secret of success. But what about being the right person? The world is abundant in opportunities, but most people aren't trained to see them. It's not enough to be in the right place at the right time. You have to be *the right person* to benefit from the circumstances. If you are the right person, you attract the right circumstances and the right people, because you intentionally shape your life.

Embrace your story. Believe in your personal power. Discover your dream. Become aware of your limitations. Work on yourself and your dream. Develop winning qualities within your personality

I challenge you to wake up each day with determination and go to bed with satisfaction.

To support you on your journey towards creating the life you dream about, please visit http://anna-simpson.com.

Finally could you please take a moment also to leave a review for me from whatever site you purchased this book. It would be so appreciated!

Anna Simpson

Acknowledgements

I would like to acknowledge Christian Simpson, Paul Martinelli, Roddy Galbraith and John Maxwell for being part of my wonderful journey of self-discovery and fulfillment.

References

"Success Principles", Jack Canfield, Janet Switser

"The Power of Now: A Guide to Spiritual Enlightment", Eckhart Tolle

"Biology of Belief", Bruce Lipton

"The Elephant and the Rope" Unknown author

"Hindus Legend" Unknown author

www.ingramcontent.com/pod-product-compliance
Lightning Source LLC
Chambersburg PA
CBHW021111080526
44587CB00010B/471